# THE ULTIMATE GUIDE
# TO BOWHUNTING

# THE ULTIMATE GUIDE TO BOWHUNTING

An essential guide for beginning and accomplished bowhunters

## H. LEA LAWRENCE

HARMONY LIBRARY
Fort Collins, Colorado

The Lyons Press
Guilford, Connecticut
An imprint of The Globe Pequot Press

The Lyons Press is an imprint of The Globe Pequot Press.

Printed in the United States of America

Designed by Compset, Inc.

10 9 8 7 6 5 4 3 2 1

Library of Congress Cataloging-in-Publication Data is available on file.

Photo credits

Ameristep: 111 (right), 113, 114 (top)
Arizona E-Z Fletch: 23 (top)
Biggins, Dean, USFWS: 76
Blue Ridge Targets: 169, 171 (right)
Browning: 2, 8, 11, 14 (right), 31 (bottom), 32 (bottom left), 34, 90 (right)
Bushnell: 92 (top)
Cabela's: 23 (bottom), 26 (bottom), 33, 46 (top), 91 (bottom), 100, 115 (right), 164 (bottom), 165
Erikson, David, USFWS: 77
Fine-Line: 32 (top left), 91 (top)
Garmin: 96 (bottom)
Gentry, George, USFWS: 64
Golden Key-Futura: 32 (bottom right), 49 (right), 89 (bottom)
Hawk Associates: 95 (bottom)
HoytUSA: 7, 10, 12
L.L. Bean: 46 (bottom), 92 (bottom), 94, 96 (top), 109, 121
McKenzie Targets: 38, 168, 170, 171 (left), 173 (top)
Menke, Dave, USFWS: 69
Mishler, Neal: 139, 147
Mossy Oak: xii, 9, 14 (left), 30, 59, 97, 105, 108, 119, 124, 129, 173 (bottom)
New Archery Products: 27, 89 (top), 90 (left)
North American Archery Group: 26 (top), 88, 140, 163
Ol' Man Treestands: 53, 111 (left), 112
Primos Hunting Calls: 106, 120, 144
PSE Archery: 13, 32 (top right), 50
Robinson Labs: 102, 103
Scent-Lok: 114 (bottom)
Spot-Hogg: 31 (top)
Trebark: 115 (right), 142
Truglo: 49 (left)
U.S. Fish & Wildlife Service: 66, 72, 74
Walker's Game Ear: 95 (top)
Watson, Aubrey: 22, 39, 40, 47, 145, 150, 164 (top)
White, Dave: 5, 41, 43, 44, 45, 98
Zahm, Gary, USFWS: 67

# DEDICATION

*This book is dedicated to the late Ben Rodgers Lee, a valued friend and woodsman without parallel, and to Bob Foulkrod, one of the world's great bowhunters with whom I have shared many exciting adventures in the U.S., Canada and Africa.*

# CONTENTS

Introduction ............................................... ix
A *brief history of the bow, its origin and uses over the centuries; the phe-nomenal growth in recent years of both archery and bowhunting.*

1) Choosing Equipment ................................. 1
*First steps: finding the master eye; the selection of the bow and arrows, importance of bow weight, matching arrows; arrows and energy; fletching; making your own arrows; selecting points; matching to draw length; accessories; equipment and instruction for youngsters.*

2) Learning to Shoot ................................... 37
*Familiarizing oneself with the equipment; the preliminary steps; proper stance; nocking; drawing, holding and aiming; release and follow-through; bowsights; improving your aim.*

3) When Things Go Wrong ........................... 51
*Ways to correct shooting faults; safety in the field and on the ranges; how proper care and use of equipment relates to safety and good performance; hypothermia and accidents.*

4) Ethics ................................................. 57
*Why ethics are of special importance to bowhunters and how individual hunters can make a difference; what to do; what not to do.*

5) Big-Game Animals ................................. 63
*The many species of big-game animals in North America sought by bowhunters; their size, characteristics, and the various places on the continent where they can be found.*

6) Hunting Big Game ................................. 83
*The confidence and skill a hunter must possess before seeking big-game animals; field dressing and utilization of meat; accessories important for a successful hunt.*

7) Tree Stands ........................................ 107
*Benefits of using stands; popular types of portable stands, including climbing, strap-on, ladder and tripod varieties.*

8) Stalking .......................................... 117
*The challenge of moving quietly through the woods; skill in using the wind; choice of clothing; importance of scouting; skills that aid productivity.*

9) Driving ........................................... 127
*Driving techniques important in bowhunting for whitetail deer. Why quiet drives are often preferred.*

10) Small Game ...................................... 131
*Advantages of small-game hunting; developing pinpoint accuracy at both stationary and moving objects; opportunity for skill building and a change of pace.*

11) The King and Other Birds ......................... 137
*The wild turkey revolution; tactics, types of calls, equipment and accessories needed; other game birds; wingshooting tips.*

12) Varmints ........................................ 153
*Year-round hunting opportunity with coyotes, bobcats, groundhogs, beaver, prairie dog, gophers, even crows; hunting strategies and tips.*

13) Fish ............................................ 161
*Methods and benefits of bowhunting fish; specialized equipment and techniques.*

14) Field Games and Archery Competitions ............. 167
*Target and field games; trends, basic rules and techniques; 3-D competition; a bowhunter's success story; NAA and NFAA events; Olympic competition; world target archery.*

Appendix A: National and International Archery and Bowhunting Organizations ....................................... 177

Appendix B: Government Regulating Agencies ............. 185

Index ................................................ 189

# INTRODUCTION

N o one knows where or when the first bow and arrow appeared, because it came into being long before recorded time. It's also possible that there was no single place of origin but that it evolved in several locations. The fact that it dates far back in time isn't disputed, and some evidence suggests that its inception may have been 100,000 or more years ago.

Some things clearly depict its early existence, though. There are paintings of archers in stone shelters in Spain that were done during the Mesolithic period approximately 10,000 years ago, and it is known that Egyptians were using bows and arrows as early as 3500 B.C. Assyrians produced the basic recurve design in 1800 B.C. that later became the model for the modern version.

But the earliest-known cave drawings, discovered in 1940 at Lascaux in southern France, clearly show a bison with seven arrows protruding from its side. These drawings are from the Paleolithic period, some 25,000 years ago.

The contribution of archery to the progress of human history was of enormous significance. The earliest men were likely primarily vegetarians, eating foods that were readily available by scrounging things such as berries, fruits, nuts and whatever small living creatures they could gather by hand or with tools no more advanced than rocks or sticks.

With a weapon capable of bringing down larger game for food or to thwart an attack, and then to have the benefits of new raw materials for various domestic uses, primitive man was able to make larger strides toward survival and a more civilized existence.

Before the time of the first ancient Olympic games around 776 B.C., archery had become a game as well as a means of self-protection and food gathering. By A.D. 500 the Romans had improved archery by developing better shooting methods and stances that led to furthering it as a competitive skill as well as a vital weapon of war. At the same time, archery skills were being highly developed in Asia, and the invaders' use of these weapons contributed to the fall of the Roman Empire.

The great stories and ballads about heroic figures like William Tell began to appear in England in A.D. 1300, and by the 17th century, archery competition was a tournament event at fairs and community festivals.

The invention of gunpowder influenced most of the civilized countries, but the use of the bow and arrow continued to play a prominent role in many of the less-developed parts of the world. The tiny, poison-tipped arrows of the African Bushmen and Pygmy tribes were vital to their existence, and for many centuries the American Indians had no other means of gathering game or defending themselves.

In America, the awareness of archery increased following the Civil War. Confederate veterans weren't permitted to own firearms, so two brothers, J. Maurice and William H. Thompson, resorted to archery as a means of gathering food. They became accomplished at this skill, and in 1879 they founded the National Archery Association at Crawfordsville, Indiana.

It was in 1900 that archery was made an official event at the Olympics, where it was also included in 1904, 1908 and 1920. This was its start as a recreational and competitive sport, and while at that time a few archers did some hunting with the bow and arrow, it was mostly on a limited scale and for small game. The first real progress in bringing bowhunting to the public's attention as a suitable and efficient means of taking all kinds of game came in the 1920s through the efforts of Saxon Pope and Art Young, who were advocates of archery for both recreation and bowhunting.

The remarkable thing is that the appeal and the romance of archery, which utilizes an essentially primitive shooting system, has not only survived the invention and development of highly sophisticated and efficient firearms but has become the nation's fastest-growing shooting sport. From a hunter's standpoint, it's quite obvious that it speaks to the most basic instincts. Saxon Pope, in *Hunting with the Bow and Arrow*, may have explained this apparent paradox best when he wrote:

"Here we have a weapon of beauty and romance. He who shoots with a bow puts his life's energy into it. The force behind the flying shaft must be placed there by the archer. At the moment of greatest strain he must draw every sinew to the utmost; his hand must·be steady; his nerves under absolute control; his eye clean and clear. In the hunt he pits his well-trained skill against the instinctive cunning of his quarry. By the most adroit cleverness, he must approach within striking distance, and when he speeds his low-whispering shaft and strikes his game, he has won by the strength of arm and nerve. It is a noble sport."

Many things contribute to the continuing popularity of all forms of archery, but the two most prominent are *opportunity* and *diversity*. In recreational archery, for example, there are many organizations and facilities available. Truly, there are few towns and cities across the nation that don't have some kind of indoor or outdoor shooting range that provides archers a variety of games.

Industry has been quick to react to the revolution in archery, and has kept pace with the growing interest by investing heavily in the development of new and more diversified equipment and accessories designed specifically for this market. Many companies have also put professional archers and bowhunters into the field to conduct seminars and instructional sessions to generate even more public interest and enthusiasm. There are many national and regional dealers and publicly attended shows dedicated strictly to archery, and the two most prominent of all dealer shows, the annual Shooting, Hunting Outdoor Trade Show (SHOT) and National Sporting Goods Association Show (NSGA), both held at the beginning of each year, serve as showplaces for all of the new products industry has to offer for archers and bowhunters. The AMO Archery Trade Show is also an annual event, and it is devoted exclusively to showcasing the best new bowhunting gear.

What has generated the most energy and enthusiasm in recent years has been the huge increase in bowhunting, and especially big game. Where at one time the use of archery tackle for the larger game species was prohibited virtually everywhere in the country (in fact, the first legal bowhunt for deer didn't occur in the U.S. until the late 1930s), today bowhunting for big game is permitted throughout the nation, and in many cases archers have longer hunting seasons than gun hunters—and sometimes larger bag limits.

Finally, the combination of recreational archery and bowhunting further enhances the sport. Many people take up archery with the main purpose of becoming a hunter. If learning required only shooting at bullseye targets to develop skill, recreational archery would soon cease offering challenges. Now, though, with exciting and complex field games that simulate hunting situations, millions of archers are extending their participation to competitive shooting and bowhunting.

This makes the future look very bright, especially for bowhunting. However, it is imperative that this increase in popularity be accompanied by a concerted effort to enlarge and expand the education programs that relate to both hunters and the general public. Remember that hunters of all kinds make up only about 10 percent of the population, and that bowhunters represent only 15 to 20 percent of that number. On the other hand, of the 90 percent of the population that doesn't hunt, about 10 percent are opposed to the sport.

In many cases, this "anti" sentiment is due largely to lack of understanding, so education and information efforts aimed at this group of people can pay significant dividends. Ultimately, though, the major responsibility for maintaining and improving the image of bowhunting lies in the hunters themselves.

Progress is being made. Most states have mandatory hunter safety programs for youths and first-time purchasers of hunting licenses. Interestingly, these sessions are often voluntarily attended by hunters with experience who want to brush up on current rules and safety measures. Seminars conducted by experts and professionals also are very effective means of educating both hunters and the general public. They deal with topics ranging from instructions for beginners to advanced hunting tactics. Individual hunter responsibility is emphasized and encouraged.

Basically stated, it comes down to this: the *tomorrow* of bowhunting will be determined by what bowhunters do *today*.

It's all up to you.

*A bowhunter brings home a trophy buck.*

# 1

# CHOOSING EQUIPMENT

In order to get the right start in archery, regardless of what form of the sport is involved—field, target or bowhunting—following some simple first steps will help avoid a lot of frustration and disappointment.

It is important that the novice first gain some knowledge of the fundamentals and realize that archery, like many other skills, requires a "crawl-before-you-walk" approach. One begins with the basics and progresses accordingly. One of the worst mistakes a beginner can make is to go out and buy a bow and some arrows and start practicing. Without any knowledge of what's recommended, it's easy to select the wrong equipment, with the result that often you'll have to unlearn everything and begin all over again. Buying equipment that is too advanced is another error beginners make. The result is similar to trying to learn to drive using a 15-speed tractor trailer truck instead of a car that has an automatic transmission and power steering.

There are several ways to go about learning the ABCs of archery. One of the best is to enlist the help of a friend who is an archer and who can help guide you to right decisions regarding basic needs and choices. Another area of assistance is through some of the excellent instructional videos, tapes and books available. Going to archery or bowhunting meets and tournaments and watching experienced archers shoot can be very helpful, too. At these events there are experts who are usually willing to answer questions and offer assistance to beginners. It's a good idea to get more than one expert's opinion, particularly on equipment items. Experienced shooters have personal preferences that may not be what's best suited for you.

Once familiar with the fundamentals, the next step is the selection of equipment, and this is a point where you can place yourself in jeopardy. No matter how much reading and observing you may have done, it's a mistake to try to personally judge what's best to begin with. Sporting goods stores, department stores and mail-order catalogs feature mind-boggling displays of equipment that can confuse experienced archers, much less beginners. Even at places where equipment can be tried out on the spot, the salesmen sometimes aren't qualified to provide expert advice.

The most effective and efficient way to get started right is to go to a pro shop. These places specialize in getting beginners under way properly by de-

*The right equipment and good advice will lead to a lifetime of great shooting.*

termining precisely the best equipment for each individual. This is done by letting the person try many different bows until one is found that feels the most comfortable to handle. Next comes the process of matching the equipment and supplying the necessary accessories. After that, the shop's specialist will monitor your progress and keep adjusting the tackle accordingly. The services of a pro shop cost a little more at the outset, but it's an expense that many experienced archers feel is well worth it in the long run.

If you happen to be in a location where there's no pro shop nearby, some of the major manufacturers of archery equipment will provide the beginner with information and assistance. Supply them with details about yourself—height, weight, age, and the type of archery activity you're interested in—and ask them to make recommendations on the kind of tackle you should purchase to start with, and the names and addresses of either nearby dealers or sales representatives who can lend additional help.

Once you have the right equipment, stick with it. Switching around and experimenting with other tackle can totally confuse and derail the learning process.

## FINDING THE MASTER EYE

The first thing a beginner must do before selecting a bow is determine his or her dominant, or "master," eye. Generally speaking, in right-handed persons the right eye is dominant, and vice versa for left-handed persons. However, there are cases where this isn't true, particularly in individuals who happen to be ambidextrous and use both hands with equal ease.

It's important to make this your first step. Occasionally, shooters start out using the wrong hand and eye and then discover later that they have to switch. This means learning all over again, and there's no use doing things the hard way when it can be easily avoided.

There are a couple of simple methods for finding out which eye is dominant. One is to hold the arms straight out and make a triangle with the thumbs and forefingers. Pick an object in the distance and focus on it. Then slowly bring the triangle closer to the face, keeping your eye on the object. The triangular opening will be drawn back to the dominant eye.

Another way is to point your finger at an object with both eyes open. Then close or cover one eye and see if the tip of the finger remains on the point of focus. If it does, the eye you are looking through is dominant. If not, then it is the other eye.

There are instances where the dominant eye is impaired or not functional. This makes it necessary for the person either to learn to shoot with the other hand, or to use a special bow sight with extended pins to compensate for the difference in point of aim.

# MODERN BOW CHOICES

Most Americans of a certain age became familiar with bows and arrows by seeing cowboy and Indian movies when they were young, and this inspired a lot of kids to fashion their own versions out of tree limbs and grocer's twine. To say the least, the toy weapons were clumsy and inefficient; but if nothing more, they provided a rudimentary idea of the principles involved. The commercial bow and arrow outfits available for youngsters then (and still available now) had arrows with rubber stoppers on the end that would stick to glass or other flat, smooth surfaces. Often youngsters wore an Indian headdress with brightly colored feathers to complete the look.

It's possible that using these toys may inspire some children to eventually take up the sport of archery. Possible, yes, yet space age weapons seem to be the preference of children today.

The most important media influences on archery in the late 1930s and early 1940s were the popular film *Robin Hood* and the movie shorts showing the fantastic archery skills of the great Howard Hill. Both of these featured the longbow, which provided the sport with a much more attractive and appealing image.

At about the same time, the legendary Fred Bear was generating interest in both recreational archery and bowhunting. His efforts launched archery, and especially bowhunting, on a course that has developed into the fastest-growing shooting sport in the nation.

## THE LONGBOW

Earlier in this century, when Saxon Pope and Art Young were in search of the best type of equipment to use for target shooting and hunting, they experimented with bows and arrows produced by seventeen different Indian tribes, as well as thirteen others that were created by bowyers in various foreign countries.

*American archery pioneers took the English longbow as their model, and it is still used by those who prefer traditional equipment for hunting and competition.*

The results showed that a 65-pound English yew longbow topped them all, sending an arrow 300 yards. Second was a 70-pound Yaki Indian bow that shot an arrow 210 yards; and third, a 56-pound Nigrito bow propelled an arrow 176 yards. This led Pope to say that this particular English bow was the most powerful artillery of its sort in the world.

Actually, the Thompson brothers mentioned in the introduction found the English longbow much more efficient than the Indian bows, so its worth had already been established by the time Pope and Young became active in trying to renew interest in the sport of archery and the attempt to modernize equipment. They added much to the knowledge of longbow construction by experimenting with different kinds of native American wood instead of the traditional English yew. They used Osage orange, mulberry, black walnut, cedar and hickory, and they discovered that Tennessee red cedar backed with hickory was a good substitute for yew. The longbows they made were among the first sophisticated hunting and target bows produced in this country, and their designs became the standard for manufacturing bows for American archers.

Another great contribution by Pope and Young was Pope's classic books, *Hunting with the Bow and Arrow* and *The Adventurous Bowmen*, published in the 1920s. They chronicled the duo's hunting adventures on the North American and African continents and their various research projects. These books inspired hunters to adopt archery as a sport that offered challenge and satisfaction both as recreation and hunting. Today's gigantic interest in all forms of archery can be largely traced to this beginning.

This classic bow hasn't disappeared from the scene, and is actually experiencing a comeback. Now instead of being a bow for the beginner, it's more often used by veteran shooters who like to return to traditional equipment because of the aesthetics. They're traditional in design, but the current models are made of fiberglass, laminated and impregnated wood, and other modern materials. Many of them, if not most, are custom built and very expensive.

## THE RECURVE BOW

Unlike the longbow, which has straight limbs and an average length of nearly 6 feet, its successor, the recurve bow, is more compact, with elongated S-curved limbs that supply more energy than straight ones, and which results in less recoil.

The modern recurve bow was made famous by Fred Bear in the early 1950s. Bear modified a bow design invented in ancient times by Turkish and Persian warriors, and used modern laminating techniques combining wood and fiberglass to create the fastest and most efficient bows ever built up to that time.

Recurves are graceful in appearance, and this type of bow still has many dedicated users, especially among instinctive shooters. Too, there are some excellent takedown recurve bows available today that are ideal for traveling or storing, and which perform equally as well as the one-piece models.

Today recurves, like longbows, are often used by experienced bowyers who started out with a compound and decided to revert to a more traditional archery form, but there are many hunters who prefer them over a compound bow for various reasons. One is that they're less complicated and are trouble-free. Another, just as important, is that with use of modern materials and advanced technology, their performance compares favorably.

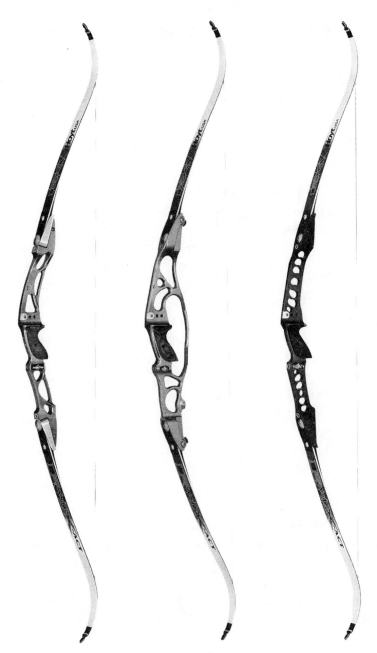

*The performance of modern recurves continues to improve.*

*One-cam bows like this one have gained fast popularity in recent years as they offer high performance and easy tuning.*

## THE COMPOUND BOW

The appearance of the first compound bows on the market in the late 1960s marked the most radical change in archery design and function in the history of the sport. By traditional standards, they were considered unsightly, but once archers overcame this reaction and began to use them, their advantages quickly became apparent. Today they dominate both the target and bowhunting markets.

The compound bow consists of two limbs made of fiberglass, graphite, foam, wood, or combinations of these materials, and a center or handle section. At each end are brackets that hold eccentric wheels and pulleys and cables that attach to the drawstring. This is a basic description, because from this have evolved some highly complex mechanisms, an immense variety of bow designs and various high-tech add-on accessories that are described in a later chapter.

What should be considered is that a good-quality compound bow is so easy to handle that it's ideal for a beginner. The main reason is that a person can start out with a bow weight that will continue to be satisfactory for target or hunting purposes as the level of skill increases. No change or upgrade is necessary.

The mechanism just described is what makes this possible. With a longbow or recurve bow, the draw weight increases as the string is pulled back, but with a compound, the weight peaks at mid-draw, then reduces as much as 65 to 80 percent as you reach full draw. It's called "let-off," and it can allow a beginning bowhunter to have a bow that will be capable of bagging medium-size big-game animals such as whitetail deer and antelope once his or her shooting skills are developed.

*Compound bows come in all sizes and configurations. Here a hunter gets ready to shoot from a tree stand.*

Two of the basic considerations in compound bow selection should be what kind of performance you prefer, and to what use it will be put. This is where wheel choice plays a part. The round wheel design has the advantage of providing a smoother draw, as well as being more dependable, efficient and less trouble to tune. Cam wheel bows are faster, but as with many other devices and mechanisms, there's a trade-off involved. The trend in recent years has been a move from two-cam designs to single-cam designs, often with shorter axle-to-axle lengths to improve maneuverability in hunting situations. The one-cam design has an oversize "hard" cam on the lower limb only and eliminates the problem of synchronization. Bowhunters can choose soft, medium and hard cams, and each fills a niche in the market. Medium cams are a nice choice for hunters looking for the best compromise in speed and performance. Bow makers are continuing to find ways to decrease vibration and noise while increasing arrow speed.

The most confusing part of bow selection for a beginner is the dizzying array of compound bows on the market that range all the way from basic, functional models to high-tech versions loaded with accessories that resemble something from outer space. Without expert or professional advice and guidance, it's easy to be diverted or influenced by cosmetics or glamour and make a bad judgment at square one.

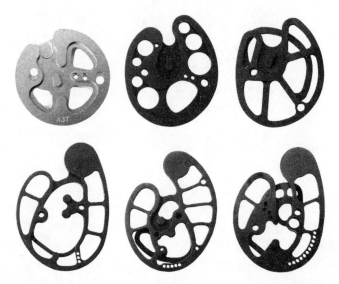

*In today's market, bowhunters can choose among many types of cams, from "soft" cams (round) that offer smooth shooting to the elliptical "hard" cams that give shooters more speed. Many hunters opt for "mid" cams that combine good speed with quiet, smooth performance.*

*Most compound bows can be purchased as full packages, with a quiver, arrow rest, bowsight, stabilizer, string silencer, and wrist sling included.*

## THE CROSSBOW

Until recently it would not have been logical to include the crossbow in the category of recreational archery, because it was legal as a hunting weapon in only a small handful of states. That situation has changed, magnifying the role of the crossbow and making it a type of equipment that some beginning archers may wish to consider.

This isn't to say that it doesn't remain controversial, and there are many archers, and particularly bowhunters, who vigorously oppose its use. Still, this has been overcome to the point that most states permit crossbows for hunting one or more different kinds of game, and further expansion of these privileges is anticipated.

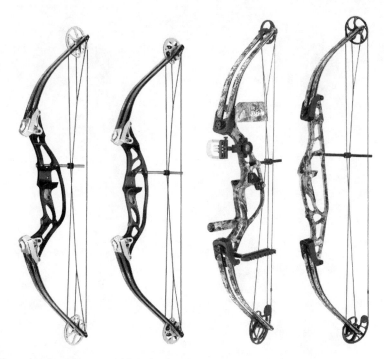

*A fine selection of target and hunting bows.*

There is a strange attitude regarding the crossbow that suggests that since it was a medieval instrument of war, it is therefore evil. This ignores the fact that the longbow, which has no such stigma attached to it, was in use at the same time. The main reason for looking askance at the crossbow, though, is that the mechanism is different. Traditional archers—as well as many users of compound bows—tend to have a purist attitude. They claim the crossbow is too much like a firearm in both appearance and function.

It's quite natural that the crossbow occupies a separate competitive shooting category, and there are in fact national organizations that include it in their schedule of events.

Crossbows initially followed the longbows and recurves as far as limb design was concerned, but the modern versions use the compound bow system. This makes it possible to bring the string back into the cocked position without the use of a lever. Crossbows are extremely powerful and can be fitted with scopes

*The compound bow principle has been added to crossbows, making them easier to cock. With a scope, they perform with great accuracy.*

that make them very accurate within the limits of their range. Incidentally, the shaft delivered by a crossbow is referred to as a bolt rather than an arrow.

As with the other types of equipment, the best source of information on crossbows and accessories will be sporting goods stores or pro shops.

## A U-TURN IN EQUIPMENT PREFERENCES

Although plenty of big-game animals had been taken in America by bowhunters before the 1960s, it was about that time that the sport became exceedingly popular. The selection of bows was limited to longbows and recurves, and the offering of accessories was somewhat meager. The fact that the sport posed more of a challenge than gun hunting held off many who were otherwise attracted to it.

That was the situation until the appearance of the compound bow, which immediately created an explosion of interest and participation. Once it began, the zeal to get more people involved in the sport resulted in manufacturers creating all sorts of gadgets intended to make bowhunting so easy that everyone from children to grandparents could participate.

Compound bows allowed millions of people to shoot bows of weights that previously would have been impossible for them to pull back to a full draw. This advanced technology also permitted inexperienced and unskilled hunters to go afield, and this in turn resulted in increased personal injuries and crippled game. In too many instances the basic elements of bowhunting were shunted aside in favor of expediency.

The trend toward simplicity persisted through the 1970s, but at the beginning of the 1980s, a reversal began to occur. Many bowhunters, some of

*Bowhunting has increased in popularity with women, and several bow manufacturers now make bows specifically designed for women shooters.*

whom had begun with traditional equipment and had moved on to compound bows, did a U-turn and reverted to longbows and recurves.

Principal among their reasons was a desire to rediscover the pleasure and satisfaction they had enjoyed when using their personal skills instead of gadgets. In a sense, it reflected the national attitudes that favored the natural instead of the artificial, as well as a willingness and even a zeal to face challenges.

Whitetail hunters constituted the majority of the "escapees." Gun seasons had become crowded to the point that solitude in the woods was impossible to experience. Early and separate bowhunting seasons offered the opportunity to get out into the woods and enjoy this simple pleasure again. There was also the appeal of a hunter facing nature with only the basics.

The first hunters to re-enter or to choose to enter the traditional fold were those who either possessed or wished to learn the multiple skills required. They liked the idea of becoming *woodsmen* rather than just *shooters*.

Something else became apparent to those who had experienced using all kinds of bows. They found that when they shot the heavier hunting arrows, quality longbows and recurve bows would do practically everything a compound bow does. The only disadvantage lies in having no breakover or holding weight or the ability to shoot lighter arrows. On the other hand, compound bows upset the rhythm enjoyed when shooting a traditional bow (which is the reason the legendary Fred Bear, the country's most famous bowhunter, never abandoned the recurve).

Evidence of this return to basics is plain to see. In 1980 there were fewer than ten custom "stick bow" builders who advertised; by 1990 the number had climbed to over seventy. This increase gained the attention of the big manufacturers, who began producing more of the kinds of equipment that traditionalists wanted, some of which they'd dropped when the rush to technology was occurring. New longbows and recurves appeared in their catalogs; and as the number of traditional hunters continued to expand, quality rather than quantity became the hallmark.

This isn't a prediction that the pendulum will swing to an opposite position, but it illustrates that as the overall increase in bowhunting continues, the ratio of compound bowhunters versus traditional bowhunters is changing.

And as a bonus, some attitudes are changing as well!

## BOW SELECTION AND BOW WEIGHT

The term "bow weight" doesn't refer to the *actual* weight of the bow, but rather to the amount of force in pounds that is required to draw an arrow to its full length. For all practical purposes, it's better to think of it as "draw weight."

In the case of longbows and recurve bows, the weight marked on them represents the poundage measured by bringing a 28-inch arrow to full draw. This is the length arrow best suited for the arm span of an average adult male. Obviously, there have to be variations in this system due to age and physical size. A person with a shorter draw length will be pulling less weight, and a longer draw will increase the weight. This is another reason for making certain your equipment is matched. You don't want to start off with a weight that's too great, because this can affect your shooting to the point that you'll likely become discouraged at seeing little progress. Worse still, it could cause you to quit the sport entirely.

Regardless of what type of equipment you choose, make sure you're comfortable with it, not just in draw weight, but also in the general "feel." The best way to determine this is with hands-on experience. Go to several stores and pro shops and try as many bows as you can until you find one that seems right.

Persons preferring to start out with a longbow or recurve bow will begin with a particular weight, then in time they will move up to a higher draw level. Pulling a bow requires the use of certain back muscles that aren't ordinarily given a workout, but with practice, they strengthen and handle more weight. The only problem is that since draw weight on longbows and recurves isn't adjustable, advancing one's skill level means sooner or later buying another bow. In the case of the takedown recurve, however, this means only purchasing another more powerful set of limbs.

Two of the biggest advantages offered by a compound bow are that both the draw length and draw weight are adjustable and can be lessened or increased as needed. This makes it possible to start with one bow and continue to use it from the basic steps in shooting all the way through to hunting big game. A compound bow pulling 45 to 60 pounds can take down most big-game animals on this continent provided the right broadhead is used and its placement is correct. The second plus is the let-off feature, which doesn't require the shooter to hold back the full bow weight at full draw.

This suggests one of the major don'ts in bow selection, which is: don't purchase too heavy a bow at the outset. The idea of being able to draw an 80- to 90-pound bow may bolster the ego, and heavier bows will project an arrow faster and with flatter trajectory. The downside is that it can also be a serious impediment to learning to shoot properly. A heavy bow is hard to hold, and as a result, accuracy suffers. Also, heavier bows are more subject to breakage, and although many companies manufacture them, they will not warranty them beyond a certain poundage.

The best plan to follow is to select a bow that is comfortable to hold and to draw. Get matched arrows and shoot until the procedure becomes almost second nature. Believe in the old saying that "practice makes perfect" and stick with it!

# ARROWS

Arrows come in a variety of materials suitable for use in any kind of bow, but they must be carefully matched to the equipment to obtain proper performance. The flight characteristic of an arrow is determined by several factors. One of these is its stiffness, or spine, the degree of which is increased by both draw weight and arrow length. An arrow with too little spine will shatter or fly erratically. Arrow weight is another consideration, since it influences trajectory, accuracy and striking power. The right kind of fletching is needed, too, and this choice has to do with the purpose for which the arrow is intended. Arrowhead weight is important, and when broadheads are used it becomes more critical because of the considerable differences in sizes and design. Finally, proper alignment of the nock and fletching assures better arrow flight. For beginners, this is another project that shouldn't be attempted without expert advice.

The arrow, like a bullet, is a projectile whose flight is launched by the release of stored energy. In the case of a rifle, the energy is in the form of gunpowder contained in the cartridge; in the bow, energy is generated and stored as the string is drawn.

In both cases, the energy is transferred to the projectile in the form of kinetic energy, which is used in its struggle through the air as it flies toward a target. If its shape is blunt, there is more air resistance, causing the velocity to drop rapidly in proportion to the remaining energy. A pointed or streamlined shape is more efficient and retains energy longer. In this sense, "velocity" is simply another method of defining energy and a way to indicate the energy remaining.

For bowhunters in particular, the most important thing is *penetration:* the hunter must make certain the arrow retains sufficient energy to accomplish this satisfactorily. Energy is vital, but the factors of arrow weight, broadhead design, type of fletching and straightness of flight are all involved. All these influence how energy is expended, and there are various tradeoffs. For example, since the use of heavy arrows for big game is recommended, adding speed means sacrificing both energy and penetration.

For those who prefer to delve into it further, there is an equation for figuring the kinetic energy of an arrow where V equals velocity:

$$\frac{V^2 \times \text{arrow weight (grains)}}{450{,}240} = \text{foot-pounds of kinetic energy}$$

Gravity and air friction affect anything moving through the atmosphere, and both begin to influence arrow flight the instant it is launched. Contrary to some opinions, arrows leaving the bow do not overcome gravity and "rise." This is an illusion, but one that's easily explained: the actual point of aim is above the spot where the arrow is intended to strike. Basically, the degree of elevation is determined by distance from the target and how the equipment performs.

As far as air friction is concerned, the best way to illustrate its effect in diminishing energy is to think about how much more effort is required of a person walking into a stiff wind.

Some bows are more efficient in transferring energy than others, and each shooter must make a choice based on experience and personal preference. Also, there's a difference between using a mechanical release and using fingers. There is a phenomenon called "archer's paradox" that refers to a bend in the arrow that occurs when it is suddenly thrust forward by the surge of stored energy. This occurs very rapidly and can't be seen by the naked eye, but it has a slight influence on velocity. The bend is more pronounced when using a finger release, since it's impossible to get fingers out of the way. The string rolls off to the right or left, according to which hand you draw with, and it takes slightly longer for the arrow to stabilize and establish a proper flight path. With the mechanical release, you get a perfect release every time, since the string goes in a straight line behind the arrow.

## MATERIALS

Matching arrows is much easier now than when wood arrows were the only choice. Wood has inherent problems in regard to weight, density, stiffness and the difficulty in manufacturing shafts with uniform straightness and circumference. Also, wood is porous and can absorb moisture, causing warping and weight increase.

The development of fiberglass, aluminum and carbon shafts has improved the ability to match arrows with much greater accuracy. And while wood is still a choice of archers who use traditional bows, it's mostly because they enjoy the aesthetics and the satisfaction of making their own arrows.

The first alternate to wood was fiberglass arrows. Tougher and stiffer than wood arrows, they could stand more abuse and were proven game-getters.

# Easton Outdoor & Indoor Target • Field • 3-D Shaft Size Selection

## Correct Arrow Length for Target • Field • 3-D

| COMPOUND BOW – Release Aid Actual or Calculated PEAK BOW WEIGHT-LBS. | | | RECURVE BOW Finger Release Actual or Calculated PEAK BOW WEIGHT-LBS. |
|---|---|---|---|
| **Soft Cam** A320 up to 210 fps, IBO up to 264 fps | **Medium** AMO 271–290 fps, IBO 265–293 fps | **Single or Hard Cam** AMO 231 fps & up, IBO 294 fps & up | |
| 28-34 LBS. (12.7-15.4 KG) | | | 17-23 LBS. (7.7-10.4 KG) |
| 34-40 LBS. (15.4-18.1 KG) | 29-35 LBS. (13.2-15.9 KG) | | 24-29 LBS. (10.9-13.2 KG) |
| 40-45 LBS. (18.1-20.4 KG) | 35-40 LBS. (15.9-18.1 KG) | 29-35 LBS. (13.2-15.9 KG) | 30-35 LBS. (13.6-15.9 KG) |
| 45-50 LBS. (20.4-22.7 KG) | 40-45 LBS. (18.1-20.4 KG) | 35-40 LBS. (15.9-18.1 KG) | 36-40 LBS. (16.3-18.1 KG) |
| 50-55 LBS. (22.7-24.9 KG) | 45-50 LBS. (20.4-22.7 KG) | 40-45 LBS. (18.1-20.4 KG) | 41-45 LBS. (18.6-20.4 KG) |
| 55-60 LBS. (24.9-27.2 KG) | 50-55 LBS. (22.7-24.9 KG) | 45-50 LBS. (20.4-22.7 KG) | 46-50 LBS. (20.9-22.7 KG) |
| 60-65 LBS. (27.2-29.5 KG) | 55-60 LBS. (24.9-27.2 KG) | 50-55 LBS. (22.7-24.9 KG) | 51-55 LBS. (23.1-24.9 KG) |
| 65-70 LBS. (29.5-31.8 KG) | 60-65 LBS. (27.2-29.5 KG) | 55-60 LBS. (24.9-27.2 KG) | 56-60 LBS. (25.4-27.2 KG) |
| 70-76 LBS. (31.8-34.5 KG) | 65-70 LBS. (29.5-31.8 KG) | 60-65 LBS. (27.2-29.5 KG) | 61-65 LBS. (27.7-29.5 KG) |
| 76-82 LBS. (34.5-37.2 KG) | 70-76 LBS. (31.8-34.5 KG) | 65-70 LBS. (29.5-31.8 KG) | 66-70 LBS. (29.9-31.8 KG) |
| 82-88 LBS. (37.2-39.9 KG) | 76-82 LBS. (34.5-37.2 KG) | 70-76 LBS. (31.8-34.5 KG) | 71-76 LBS. (32.2-34.5 KG) |

Column headings for arrow length (inches): 23", 24", 25", 26", 27", 28", 29", 30", 31", 32" (with intermediate columns for Shaft Size and Shaft Weight).

SEE YOUTH RECURVE SHAFT SELECTION CHART ON PAGE 10 FOR YOUTH SIZES.

This chart set up using release aid. Compound bows use 42" wingbase axis, 65% AMO wheff + fast Flight™ type strings.

The following apply when using:
Aluminum & X7 shafts
ACE & X10 shafts: Medium point weight ACE & X10. Recommended point or Aluminum shafts.
If your equipment is set up differently, see "Calculator" section on page 9 to determine your Calculated Peak Bow Weight before using this chart.

**Selecting Cams**—Due to the many varieties of cams offered by bow manufacturers, it may be more accurate to select the correct cam by using the manufacturer's velocity rating. Some manufacturers use the AMO standard (60# peak wt., 540 gr. arrow, 30" draw) and some use the IBO standard (70# peak wt., 350 gr. arrow, 30" draw) to rate their bows. Both velocity ratings are listed in the chart under the appropriate style of cam.

For one-cam bows use the shape of the cam, not the idler wheel, to determine the correct column, or use the manufacturer's velocity rating.

**Tuning**—The chart indicates that more than one shaft size may shoot well from your bow. You may decide to shoot a lighter shaft for speed, or a heavier shaft for greater durability and penetration. Also, large variations in shooting style, bow efficiency, type of wheels or cams, bow length, string material, and type of release may require special bow tuning or a shaft size change. In these cases, you'll need to experiment and use stiffer or weaker spined shafts to fit your situation.

See Easton's Arrow Tuning and Maintenance Guide for additional information on tuning.

**"Shaft Size"** column—indicates suggested shaft sizes.

**"Shaft Model"** column—designates arrow model.
**"S"** = XX78®: Super SlamSelect®, and Super Slam® shafts (7178-T9 alloy)
**"75"** = XX75®: Yukon™, Platinum®, Legacy®, Camo Hunter®, Advantage®, Break-Up™, GameGetter®, GameGetter®II, and Jazz™ (7075-T9 alloy)
**"A/C/C®"** = Aluminum/Carbon/Composite shafts
**"Rdln"** = Redline™ Carbon Composite Shafts
**"Evln"** = Evolution™ Carbon Composite Camouflage Shafts

**"Shaft Weight"** column—indicates shaft weight only. To determine the total arrow weight, add the weights of the shaft, point, insert, UNI Bushing, nock and fletching. Where two aluminum shaft models are shown for one size, the weight listed is for XX75. Letter codes A, B, and C listed to the right of the shaft weight indicate the relative stiffness of each aluminum shaft within that "Shaft Size" box ("A" being the stiffest, "B" less stiff, etc.).

**Insert Weights—If you shoot one of the sizes listed below and use an aluminum RPS insert, add to your point weight the extra weight indicated to compensate for the heavier, tapered-shoulder inserts.**

- **2312, 2314, 2315, 2317, 2412, 2413, 2415, and 2419—add 15 grains**
- **2512 and 2514—add 30 grains**
- **2613—add 35 grains**

**FOR ARROW LENGTHS LONGER THAN 33":** From your bow weight row, move down one row in the 33" column for each inch your arrow is longer than 33".

**FOR ARROW LENGTHS SHORTER THAN 23":** From your bow weight row, move up one row in the 23" column for each inch your arrow is shorter than 23".

**FOR BOW WEIGHTS HEAVIER THAN INDICATED ON THE CHART:** From your arrow length column, move to the right one column (1" longer shaft) for each 6 lbs. your bow is heavier than the maximum weights shown.

**FOR COMPOUND BOWS WITH FINGER RELEASE:** From your bow weight row, move 1 row heavier (1 row down).

**BOWHUNTING WITH CARBON SHAFTS:** Carbon arrows may be used for hunting if special precautions are taken. See your dealer or the information packed with Easton's A/C/C, Redline, and Evolution shafts.

WARNING: Arrows must be carefully inspected before each shot to see that they have not been damaged. Shooting a damaged arrow could cause it to break and could result in injury.

# Easton Hunting Shaft Size Selection Chart

This chart was set up using: • Recurve bows with finger release • Compound bows over 42" with release aids, 65% AMO letoff • Fast Flight® type strings.
If your equipment is set up differently, see the "Variables" section on page 25 to determine your Calculated Peak Bow Weight before using this chart.

## COMPOUND BOW – Release Aid

Actual or Calculated PEAK BOW WEIGHT-LBS.

**Soft Cam** AMO up to 210 fps, IBO up to 260 fps — **Medium Cam** AMO 211–230 fps, IBO 261–290 fps — **Single or Hard Cam** AMO 231 fps up, IBO 291 fps up

Broadhead or Field Point Wt. Only

## RECURVE BOW

**Finger Release**

Actual or Calculated PEAK BOW WEIGHT-LBS.

Broadhead or Field Point Wt. Only

## Correct Arrow Length for Hunting

| Soft Cam 75 (grains 65-85) | Soft Cam 100 (grains 90-110) | Soft Cam 125 (grains 115-135) | Soft Cam 150 (grains 140-160) | Medium Cam 75 (grains 65-85) | Medium Cam 100 (grains 90-110) | Medium Cam 125 (grains 115-135) | Medium Cam 150 (grains 140-160) | Single or Hard Cam 75 (grains 65-85) | Single or Hard Cam 100 (grains 90-110) | Single or Hard Cam 125 (grains 115-135) | Single or Hard Cam 150 (grains 140-160) | 22½"-23"-23½" Shaft Size | 23" Shaft Model | 23" Shaft Weight | 23½"-24"-24½" Shaft Size | 24" Shaft Model | 24" Shaft Weight | 24½"-25"-25½" Shaft Size | 25" Shaft Model | 25" Shaft Weight | 25½"-26"-26½" Shaft Size | 26" Shaft Model | 26" Shaft Weight | 26½"-27"-27½" Shaft Size | 27" Shaft Model | 27" Shaft Weight | 27½"-28"-28½" Shaft Size | 28" Shaft Model | 28" Shaft Weight | 28½"-29"-29½" Shaft Size | 29" Shaft Model | 29" Shaft Weight | 29½"-30"-30½" Shaft Size | 30" Shaft Model | 30" Shaft Weight | 30½"-31"-31½" Shaft Size | 31" Shaft Model | 31" Shaft Weight | 31½"-32"-32½" Shaft Size | 32" Shaft Model | 32" Shaft Weight | 32½"-33"-33½" Shaft Size | 33" Shaft Model | 33" Shaft Weight | Recurve 75 (grains 65-85) | Recurve 100 (grains 90-110) | Recurve 125 (grains 115-135) | Recurve 150 (grains 140-160) |
|---|---|---|---|---|---|---|---|---|---|---|---|---|---|---|---|---|---|---|---|---|---|---|---|---|---|---|---|---|---|---|---|---|---|---|---|---|---|---|---|---|---|---|---|---|---|---|---|---|
| 45 to 50 | 42 to 47 | 39 to 44 | 36 to 41 | 40 to 45 | 37 to 42 | 34 to 39 | 31 to 36 | 35 to 40 | 32 to 37 | 29 to 34 | 24 to 31 | | | | 1913<br>1716 | 75<br>75 | 189 A<br>217 B | 1913<br>1816 | 75<br>75 | 208 A<br>222 B | 1913<br>1816 | 75<br>75 | 217 A<br>241 B | 2013<br>1916<br>3L-18 | 75<br>75<br>A/C/C | 243 A<br>271 B<br>201 | 2013<br>1916<br>3L-18 | 75<br>75<br>A/C/C | 252 A<br>281 B<br>209 | 2113<br>2016<br>3-18 | 75<br>75<br>A/C/C | 270 B<br>306 A<br>226 | 2212<br>2114<br>2016<br>2115<br>2018<br>3-28<br>500<br>520 | S<br>S,75<br>75<br>75<br>75<br>A/C/C<br>Evln<br>Rdln | 265 B<br>296 B<br>317 C<br>323 A<br>369 A<br>243<br>273<br>215 | 2212<br>2213<br>2114<br>2115<br>2018<br>3-28<br>500<br>520 | S<br>S,75<br>S,75<br>75<br>75<br>A/C/C<br>Evln<br>Rdln | 274 C<br>305 A<br>306 C<br>333 B<br>381 B<br>251<br>282<br>222 | 2312<br>2213<br>2215<br>2117<br>2020<br>3-39<br>400<br>460 | S<br>S,75<br>S,75<br>S,75<br>75<br>A/C/C<br>Evln<br>Rdln | 303 B<br>315 C<br>341 B<br>385 A<br>432 B<br>275<br>304<br>233 | 2412<br>2314<br>2215<br>2117<br>2216<br>3-49<br>400<br>410 | S<br>S,75<br>S,75<br>S,75<br>S,75<br>A/C/C<br>Evln<br>Rdln | 319 A<br>352 A<br>352 C<br>397 B<br>397 A<br>291<br>314<br>260 | 35 to 40 | 32 to 37 | 29 to 34 | 26 to 31 |
| 50 to 55 | 47 to 52 | 44 to 49 | 41 to 46 | 45 to 50 | 42 to 47 | 39 to 44 | 36 to 41 | 40 to 45 | 37 to 42 | 34 to 39 | 31 to 36 | 1913<br>1716 | 75<br>75 | 181 A<br>208 B | 1913<br>1816 | 75<br>75 | 200 A<br>223 B | 1913<br>1816 | 75<br>75 | 208 A<br>222 B | 2013<br>1916<br>3L-18 | 75<br>75<br>A/C/C | 234 A<br>261 B<br>194 | 2013<br>1916<br>3L-18 | 75<br>75<br>A/C/C | 243 A<br>271 B<br>201 | 2113<br>2016<br>3-18 | 75<br>75<br>A/C/C | 260 B<br>298 A<br>219 | 2212<br>2114<br>2016<br>2115<br>2018<br>3-28<br>500<br>520 | S<br>S,75<br>75<br>75<br>75<br>A/C/C<br>Evln<br>Rdln | 258 B<br>286 B<br>306 C<br>312 A<br>356 A<br>235<br>264<br>208 | 2212<br>2213<br>2114<br>2115<br>2018<br>3-28<br>500<br>520 | S<br>S,75<br>S,75<br>75<br>75<br>A/C/C<br>Evln<br>Rdln | 265 C<br>295 A<br>296 C<br>323 B<br>369 B<br>243<br>273<br>215 | 2312<br>2213<br>2215<br>2117<br>2020<br>3-39<br>400<br>460 | S<br>S,75<br>S,75<br>S,75<br>75<br>A/C/C<br>Evln<br>Rdln | 294 B<br>306 C<br>331 B<br>373 A<br>418 B<br>266<br>295<br>226 | 2412<br>2314<br>2215<br>2117<br>2216<br>3-49<br>400<br>410 | S<br>S,75<br>S,75<br>S,75<br>S,75<br>A/C/C<br>Evln<br>Rdln | 309 A<br>341 A<br>341 C<br>386 B<br>385 A<br>289<br>304<br>252 | 2413<br>2314<br>2315<br>2216<br>2219<br>3-49<br>400<br>410 | S,75<br>S,75<br>S,75<br>S,75<br>S,75<br>A/C/C<br>Evln<br>Rdln | 344 A<br>352 B<br>385 A<br>397 B<br>454 A<br>291<br>314<br>260 | 40 to 45 | 37 to 42 | 34 to 39 | 31 to 36 |
| 55 to 60 | 52 to 57 | 49 to 54 | 46 to 51 | 50 to 55 | 47 to 52 | 44 to 49 | 41 to 46 | 45 to 50 | 42 to 47 | 39 to 44 | 36 to 41 | 1913<br>1816 | 75<br>75 | 192 A<br>213 B | 1913<br>1816 | 75<br>75 | 200 A<br>223 B | 2013<br>1916<br>3L-18 | 75<br>75<br>A/C/C | 225 A<br>251 B<br>167 | 2013<br>1916<br>3L-18 | 75<br>75<br>A/C/C | 234 A<br>261 B<br>194 | 2113<br>2016<br>3-18 | 75<br>75<br>A/C/C | 251 B<br>285 A<br>211 | 2212<br>2114<br>2016<br>2115<br>2018<br>3-28<br>500<br>520 | S<br>S,75<br>75<br>75<br>75<br>A/C/C<br>Evln<br>Rdln | 247 B<br>278 B<br>296 C<br>301 A<br>344 A<br>227<br>256<br>201 | 2212<br>2213<br>2114<br>2115<br>2018<br>3-28<br>500<br>520 | S<br>S,75<br>S,75<br>75<br>75<br>A/C/C<br>Evln<br>Rdln | 256 C<br>285 A<br>286 C<br>312 B<br>356 B<br>235<br>264<br>208 | 2312<br>2213<br>2215<br>2117<br>2020<br>3-39<br>400<br>460 | S<br>S,75<br>S,75<br>S,75<br>75<br>A/C/C<br>Evln<br>Rdln | 284 B<br>295 C<br>320 B<br>361 A<br>405 B<br>257<br>285<br>218 | 2412<br>2314<br>2215<br>2117<br>2216<br>3-49<br>400<br>410 | S<br>S,75<br>S,75<br>S,75<br>S,75<br>A/C/C<br>Evln<br>Rdln | 299 A<br>331 A<br>331 C<br>373 B<br>373 A<br>274<br>295<br>245 | 2413<br>2314<br>2315<br>2216<br>2219<br>3-49<br>400<br>410 | S,75<br>S,75<br>S,75<br>S,75<br>S,75<br>A/C/C<br>Evln<br>Rdln | 333 A<br>341 B<br>373 A<br>386 B<br>441 A<br>283<br>304<br>252 | 2512<br>2413<br>2315<br>2415<br>2219<br>3-60<br>340<br>360 | S<br>S,75<br>S,75<br>S<br>S,75<br>A/C/C<br>Evln<br>Rdln | 330 A<br>343 B<br>385 B<br>404 A<br>454 B<br>312<br>340<br>276 | 45 to 50 | 42 to 47 | 39 to 44 | 36 to 41 |
| 60 to 65 | 57 to 62 | 54 to 59 | 51 to 56 | 55 to 60 | 52 to 57 | 49 to 54 | 46 to 51 | 50 to 55 | 47 to 52 | 44 to 49 | 41 to 46 | 1913<br>1816 | 75<br>75 | 192 A<br>213 B | 2013<br>1916<br>3L-18 | 75<br>75<br>A/C/C | 216 A<br>241 B<br>179 | 2013<br>1916<br>3L-18 | 75<br>75<br>A/C/C | 225 A<br>251 B<br>167 | 2113<br>2016<br>3-18 | 75<br>75<br>A/C/C | 242 B<br>275 A<br>203 | 2212<br>2114<br>2016<br>2115<br>2018<br>3-28<br>500<br>520 | S<br>S,75<br>75<br>75<br>75<br>A/C/C<br>Evln<br>Rdln | 239 B<br>266 B<br>285 C<br>298 A<br>332 A<br>218<br>246<br>194 | 2212<br>2213<br>2114<br>2115<br>2018<br>3-28<br>500<br>520 | S<br>S,75<br>S,75<br>75<br>75<br>A/C/C<br>Evln<br>Rdln | 247 C<br>275 A<br>276 C<br>301 B<br>344 B<br>227<br>255<br>201 | 2312<br>2213<br>2215<br>2117<br>2020<br>3-39<br>400<br>460 | S<br>S,75<br>S,75<br>S,75<br>75<br>A/C/C<br>Evln<br>Rdln | 275 B<br>285 C<br>309 B<br>348 A<br>391 B<br>249<br>276<br>211 | 2412<br>2314<br>2215<br>2117<br>2216<br>3-49<br>400<br>410 | S<br>S,75<br>S,75<br>S,75<br>S,75<br>A/C/C<br>Evln<br>Rdln | 290 A<br>320 A<br>320 C<br>361 B<br>361 A<br>265<br>285<br>237 | 2413<br>2314<br>2315<br>2216<br>2219<br>3-49<br>400<br>410 | S,75<br>S,75<br>S,75<br>S,75<br>S,75<br>A/C/C<br>Evln<br>Rdln | 323 A<br>331 B<br>362 A<br>373 B<br>427 A<br>274<br>295<br>245 | 2512<br>2413<br>2315<br>2415<br>2219<br>3-60<br>340<br>360 | S<br>S,75<br>S,75<br>S<br>S,75<br>A/C/C<br>Evln<br>Rdln | 329 A<br>339 B<br>373 B<br>392 A<br>441 B<br>302<br>330<br>267 | 2512<br>2315<br>2415<br>2219<br>3-60<br>340<br>360 | S<br>S,75<br>S<br>S,75<br>A/C/C<br>Evln<br>Rdln | 330 A<br>385 B<br>404 A<br>454 B<br>312<br>340<br>276 | 50 to 55 | 47 to 52 | 44 to 49 | 41 to 46 |
| 65 to 70 | 62 to 67 | 59 to 64 | 56 to 61 | 60 to 65 | 57 to 62 | 54 to 59 | 51 to 56 | 55 to 60 | 52 to 57 | 49 to 54 | 46 to 51 | 2013<br>1916<br>3L-18 | 75<br>75<br>A/C/C | 207 A<br>231 B<br>172 | 2013<br>1916<br>3L-18 | 75<br>75<br>A/C/C | 216 A<br>241 B<br>179 | 2113<br>2016<br>3-18 | 75<br>75<br>A/C/C | 233 B<br>264 A<br>195 | 2212<br>2114<br>2016<br>2115<br>2018<br>3-28<br>500<br>520 | S<br>S,75<br>75<br>75<br>75<br>A/C/C<br>Evln<br>Rdln | 230 B<br>256 B<br>275 C<br>280 A<br>319 A<br>210<br>237<br>186 | 2212<br>2213<br>2114<br>2115<br>2018<br>3-28<br>500<br>520 | S<br>S,75<br>S,75<br>75<br>75<br>A/C/C<br>Evln<br>Rdln | 239 C<br>266 A<br>266 C<br>298 B<br>332 B<br>218<br>246<br>194 | 2312<br>2213<br>2215<br>2117<br>2020<br>3-39<br>400<br>460 | S<br>S,75<br>S,75<br>S,75<br>75<br>A/C/C<br>Evln<br>Rdln | 265 B<br>275 C<br>299 B<br>336 A<br>378 B<br>240<br>268<br>204 | 2412<br>2314<br>2215<br>2117<br>2216<br>3-49<br>400<br>410 | S<br>S,75<br>S,75<br>S,75<br>S,75<br>A/C/C<br>Evln<br>Rdln | 280 A<br>309 A<br>309 C<br>348 B<br>348 A<br>256<br>276<br>229 | 2413<br>2314<br>2315<br>2216<br>2219<br>3-49<br>400<br>410 | S,75<br>S,75<br>S,75<br>S,75<br>S,75<br>A/C/C<br>Evln<br>Rdln | 312 A<br>320 B<br>350 A<br>361 B<br>413 A<br>265<br>285<br>237 | 2512<br>2413<br>2315<br>2415<br>2219<br>3-60<br>340<br>360 | S<br>S,75<br>S,75<br>S<br>S,75<br>A/C/C<br>Evln<br>Rdln | 319 A<br>322 B<br>362 B<br>380 A<br>427 B<br>293<br>319<br>259 | 2512<br>2315<br>2415<br>2219<br>3-60<br>340<br>360 | S<br>S,75<br>S<br>S,75<br>A/C/C<br>Evln<br>Rdln | 329 A<br>373 B<br>392 A<br>441 B<br>302<br>330<br>267 | 2512<br>2514<br>2317<br>3-71<br>300 | S<br>S,75<br>S,75<br>A/C/C<br>Evln | 330 B<br>374 A<br>438 A<br>327<br>360 | 55 to 60 | 52 to 57 | 49 to 54 | 46 to 51 |
| 70 to 76 | 67 to 73 | 64 to 70 | 61 to 67 | 65 to 70 | 62 to 67 | 59 to 64 | 56 to 61 | 60 to 65 | 57 to 62 | 54 to 59 | 51 to 56 | 2013<br>1916<br>3L-18 | 75<br>75<br>A/C/C | 207 A<br>231 B<br>172 | 2113<br>2016<br>3-18 | 75<br>75<br>A/C/C | 223 B<br>253 A<br>187 | 2212<br>2114<br>2016<br>2115<br>2018<br>3-28<br>500<br>520 | S<br>S,75<br>75<br>75<br>75<br>A/C/C<br>Evln<br>Rdln | 221 B<br>246 B<br>264 C<br>269 A<br>307 A<br>202<br>228<br>179 | 2212<br>2213<br>2114<br>2115<br>2018<br>3-28<br>500<br>520 | S<br>S,75<br>S,75<br>75<br>75<br>A/C/C<br>Evln<br>Rdln | 230 C<br>256 A<br>256 C<br>280 B<br>319 B<br>210<br>237<br>186 | 2312<br>2213<br>2215<br>2117<br>2020<br>3-39<br>400<br>460 | S<br>S,75<br>S,75<br>S,75<br>75<br>A/C/C<br>Evln<br>Rdln | 256 B<br>265 C<br>288 B<br>324 A<br>364 B<br>232<br>257<br>197 | 2412<br>2314<br>2215<br>2117<br>2216<br>3-49<br>400<br>410 | S<br>S,75<br>S,75<br>S,75<br>S,75<br>A/C/C<br>Evln<br>Rdln | 270 A<br>299 A<br>299 C<br>338 B<br>338 A<br>247<br>266<br>221 | 2413<br>2314<br>2315<br>2216<br>2219<br>3-49<br>400<br>410 | S,75<br>S,75<br>S,75<br>S,75<br>S,75<br>A/C/C<br>Evln<br>Rdln | 302 A<br>309 B<br>338 A<br>348 B<br>399 A<br>256<br>276<br>229 | 2512<br>2413<br>2315<br>2415<br>2219<br>3-60<br>340<br>360 | S<br>S,75<br>S,75<br>S<br>S,75<br>A/C/C<br>Evln<br>Rdln | 308 A<br>312 B<br>350 B<br>368 A<br>413 B<br>284<br>309<br>251 | 2512<br>2315<br>2415<br>2219<br>3-60<br>340<br>360 | S<br>S,75<br>S<br>S,75<br>A/C/C<br>Evln<br>Rdln | 319 A<br>362 B<br>380 A<br>427 B<br>293<br>319<br>259 | 2512<br>2514<br>2317<br>3-71<br>300 | S<br>S,75<br>S,75<br>A/C/C<br>Evln | 329 B<br>363 A<br>424 A<br>317<br>349 | 2514<br>2613<br>2317<br>2419<br>3-71<br>300 | S,75<br>S<br>S,75<br>75<br>A/C/C<br>Evln | 374 B<br>379 A<br>438 B<br>480 A<br>327<br>360 | 60 to 65 | 57 to 62 | 54 to 59 | 51 to 56 |
| 76 to 82 | 73 to 79 | 70 to 76 | 67 to 73 | 70 to 76 | 67 to 73 | 64 to 70 | 61 to 67 | 65 to 70 | 62 to 67 | 59 to 64 | 56 to 61 | 2113<br>2016<br>3-18 | 75<br>75<br>A/C/C | 214 B<br>243 A<br>180 | 2212<br>2114<br>2016<br>2115<br>2018<br>3-28<br>500<br>520 | S<br>S,75<br>75<br>75<br>75<br>A/C/C<br>Evln<br>Rdln | 212 B<br>237 B<br>253 C<br>258 A<br>295 A<br>194<br>218<br>172 | 2212<br>2213<br>2114<br>2115<br>2018<br>3-28<br>500<br>520 | S<br>S,75<br>S,75<br>75<br>75<br>A/C/C<br>Evln<br>Rdln | 221 C<br>246 A<br>246 C<br>269 B<br>307 B<br>202<br>228<br>179 | 2312<br>2213<br>2215<br>2117<br>2020<br>3-39<br>400<br>460 | S<br>S,75<br>S,75<br>S,75<br>75<br>A/C/C<br>Evln<br>Rdln | 246 B<br>256 C<br>277 B<br>312 A<br>351 B<br>223<br>247<br>189 | 2412<br>2314<br>2215<br>2117<br>2216<br>3-49<br>400<br>410 | S<br>S,75<br>S,75<br>S,75<br>S,75<br>A/C/C<br>Evln<br>Rdln | 261 A<br>288 A<br>288 C<br>324 B<br>324 A<br>238<br>257<br>213 | 2413<br>2314<br>2315<br>2216<br>2219<br>3-49<br>400<br>410 | S,75<br>S,75<br>S,75<br>S,75<br>S,75<br>A/C/C<br>Evln<br>Rdln | 292 A<br>299 B<br>327 A<br>338 B<br>386 A<br>247<br>266<br>221 | 2512<br>2413<br>2315<br>2415<br>2219<br>3-60<br>340<br>360 | S<br>S,75<br>S,75<br>S<br>S,75<br>A/C/C<br>Evln<br>Rdln | 298 A<br>302 B<br>336 B<br>355 A<br>399 B<br>274<br>299<br>242 | 2512<br>2315<br>2415<br>2219<br>3-60<br>340<br>360 | S<br>S,75<br>S<br>S,75<br>A/C/C<br>Evln<br>Rdln | 308 A<br>350 B<br>368 A<br>413 B<br>284<br>309<br>251 | 2512<br>2514<br>2317<br>3-71<br>300 | S<br>S,75<br>S,75<br>A/C/C<br>Evln | 319 B<br>351 A<br>411 A<br>308<br>338 | 2514<br>2613<br>2317<br>2419<br>3-71<br>300 | S,75<br>S<br>S,75<br>75<br>A/C/C<br>Evln | 363 B<br>368 A<br>424 B<br>466 A<br>317<br>349 | 2514<br>2613<br>2317<br>2419<br>3-71<br>300 | S,75<br>S<br>S,75<br>75<br>A/C/C<br>Evln | 374 B<br>379 A<br>438 B<br>480 A<br>327<br>360 | 65 to 70 | 62 to 67 | 59 to 64 | 56 to 61 |
| 82 to 88 | 79 to 85 | 76 to 82 | 73 to 79 | 76 to 82 | 73 to 79 | 70 to 76 | 67 to 73 | 70 to 76 | 67 to 73 | 64 to 70 | 61 to 67 | 2212<br>2114<br>2016<br>2115<br>2018<br>3-28<br>500<br>520 | S<br>S,75<br>75<br>75<br>75<br>A/C/C<br>Evln<br>Rdln | 203 B<br>227 B<br>243 C<br>247 A<br>283 A<br>186<br>209<br>165 | 2212<br>2213<br>2114<br>2115<br>2018<br>3-28<br>500<br>520 | S<br>S,75<br>S,75<br>75<br>75<br>A/C/C<br>Evln<br>Rdln | 212 C<br>236 A<br>237 C<br>258 B<br>295 B<br>194<br>218<br>172 | 2312<br>2213<br>2215<br>2117<br>2020<br>3-39<br>400<br>460 | S<br>S,75<br>S,75<br>S,75<br>75<br>A/C/C<br>Evln<br>Rdln | 237 B<br>246 C<br>267 B<br>300 A<br>337 B<br>215<br>238<br>182 | 2412<br>2314<br>2215<br>2117<br>2216<br>3-49<br>400<br>410 | S<br>S,75<br>S,75<br>S,75<br>S,75<br>A/C/C<br>Evln<br>Rdln | 251 A<br>277 A<br>277 C<br>312 B<br>312 A<br>230<br>247<br>205 | 2413<br>2314<br>2315<br>2216<br>2219<br>3-49<br>400<br>410 | S,75<br>S,75<br>S,75<br>S,75<br>S,75<br>A/C/C<br>Evln<br>Rdln | 261 A<br>288 B<br>315 A<br>324 B<br>372 A<br>238<br>257<br>213 | 2512<br>2413<br>2315<br>2415<br>2219<br>3-60<br>340<br>360 | S<br>S,75<br>S,75<br>S<br>S,75<br>A/C/C<br>Evln<br>Rdln | 268 A<br>291 B<br>327 B<br>343 A<br>386 B<br>265<br>288<br>234 | 2512<br>2315<br>2415<br>2219<br>3-60<br>340<br>360 | S<br>S,75<br>S<br>S,75<br>A/C/C<br>Evln<br>Rdln | 298 A<br>338 B<br>355 A<br>399 B<br>274<br>299<br>242 | 2512<br>2514<br>2317<br>3-71<br>300 | S<br>S,75<br>S,75<br>A/C/C<br>Evln | 308 B<br>340 A<br>398 A<br>298<br>327 | 2514<br>2613<br>2317<br>2419<br>3-71<br>300 | S,75<br>S<br>S,75<br>75<br>A/C/C<br>Evln | 351 B<br>358 A<br>411 B<br>451 A<br>308<br>338 | 2514<br>2613<br>2317<br>2419<br>3-71<br>300 | S,75<br>S<br>S,75<br>75<br>A/C/C<br>Evln | 363 B<br>368 A<br>424 B<br>466 A<br>317<br>349 | 2613<br>2419 | S<br>75 | 379 A<br>480 B | 70 to 76 | 67 to 73 | 64 to 70 | 61 to 67 |
| 88 to 94 | 85 to 91 | 82 to 88 | 79 to 85 | 82 to 88 | 79 to 85 | 76 to 82 | 73 to 79 | 76 to 82 | 73 to 79 | 70 to 76 | 67 to 73 | 2212<br>2213<br>2114<br>2115<br>2018<br>3-28<br>500<br>520 | S<br>S,75<br>S,75<br>75<br>75<br>A/C/C<br>Evln<br>Rdln | 203 C<br>226 A<br>227 C<br>247 B<br>283 B<br>186<br>209<br>165 | 2312<br>2213<br>2215<br>2117<br>2020<br>3-39<br>400<br>460 | S<br>S,75<br>S,75<br>S,75<br>75<br>A/C/C<br>Evln<br>Rdln | 227 B<br>236 C<br>256 B<br>288 A<br>324 B<br>206<br>228<br>175 | 2412<br>2314<br>2215<br>2117<br>2216<br>3-49<br>400<br>410 | S<br>S,75<br>S,75<br>S,75<br>S,75<br>A/C/C<br>Evln<br>Rdln | 241 A<br>267 A<br>267 C<br>300 B<br>300 A<br>221<br>238<br>197 | 2413<br>2314<br>2315<br>2216<br>2219<br>3-49<br>400<br>410 | S,75<br>S,75<br>S,75<br>S,75<br>S,75<br>A/C/C<br>Evln<br>Rdln | 271 A<br>277 B<br>303 A<br>312 B<br>358 A<br>230<br>247<br>205 | 2512<br>2413<br>2315<br>2415<br>2219<br>3-60<br>340<br>360 | S<br>S,75<br>S,75<br>S<br>S,75<br>A/C/C<br>Evln<br>Rdln | 277 A<br>281 B<br>315 B<br>331 A<br>372 B<br>255<br>278<br>225 | 2512<br>2315<br>2415<br>2219<br>3-60<br>340<br>360 | S<br>S,75<br>S<br>S,75<br>A/C/C<br>Evln<br>Rdln | 288 A<br>327 B<br>343 A<br>386 B<br>265<br>288<br>234 | 2512<br>2514<br>2317<br>3-71<br>300 | S<br>S,75<br>S,75<br>A/C/C<br>Evln | 298 B<br>329 A<br>365 A<br>298<br>316 | 2514<br>2613<br>2317<br>2419<br>3-71<br>300 | S,75<br>S<br>S,75<br>75<br>A/C/C<br>Evln | 340 B<br>345 A<br>398 B<br>437 A<br>298<br>327 | 2514<br>2613<br>2317<br>2419<br>3-71<br>300 | S,75<br>S<br>S,75<br>75<br>A/C/C<br>Evln | 351 B<br>356 A<br>411 B<br>451 A<br>308<br>338 | 2613<br>2419 | S<br>75 | 368 A<br>466 B | 2613 | S | 379 | 76 to 82 | 73 to 79 | 70 to 76 | 67 to 73 |
| 94 to 100 | 91 to 97 | 88 to 94 | 85 to 91 | 88 to 94 | 85 to 91 | 82 to 88 | 79 to 85 | 82 to 88 | 79 to 85 | 76 to 82 | 73 to 79 | 2312<br>2213<br>2215<br>2117<br>2020<br>3-39<br>400<br>460 | S<br>S,75<br>S,75<br>S,75<br>75<br>A/C/C<br>Evln<br>Rdln | 218 B<br>226 C<br>245 B<br>276 A<br>310 B<br>197<br>219<br>167 | 2412<br>2314<br>2215<br>2117<br>2216<br>3-49<br>400<br>410 | S<br>S,75<br>S,75<br>S,75<br>S,75<br>A/C/C<br>Evln<br>Rdln | 232 A<br>256 A<br>256 C<br>288 B<br>288 A<br>212<br>228<br>189 | 2413<br>2314<br>2315<br>2216<br>2219<br>3-49<br>400<br>410 | S,75<br>S,75<br>S,75<br>S,75<br>S,75<br>A/C/C<br>Evln<br>Rdln | 260 A<br>267 B<br>292 A<br>300 B<br>344 A<br>221<br>238<br>197 | 2512<br>2413<br>2315<br>2415<br>2219<br>3-60<br>340<br>360 | S<br>S,75<br>S,75<br>S<br>S,75<br>A/C/C<br>Evln<br>Rdln | 267 A<br>270 B<br>303 B<br>319 A<br>358 B<br>246<br>268<br>217 | 2512<br>2315<br>2415<br>2219<br>3-60<br>340<br>360 | S<br>S,75<br>S<br>S,75<br>A/C/C<br>Evln<br>Rdln | 277 A<br>315 B<br>331 A<br>372 B<br>255<br>278<br>225 | 2512<br>2514<br>2317<br>3-71<br>300 | S<br>S,75<br>S,75<br>A/C/C<br>Evln | 288 B<br>317 A<br>371 A<br>278<br>305 | 2514<br>2613<br>2317<br>2419<br>3-71<br>300 | S,75<br>S<br>S,75<br>75<br>A/C/C<br>Evln | 329 B<br>333 A<br>365 B<br>422 A<br>298<br>316 | 2514<br>2613<br>2317<br>2419<br>3-71<br>300 | S,75<br>S<br>S,75<br>75<br>A/C/C<br>Evln | 340 B<br>345 A<br>398 B<br>437 A<br>298<br>327 | 2613<br>2419 | S<br>75 | 356 A<br>451 B | 2613 | S | 366 | | | | 82 to 88 | 79 to 85 | 76 to 82 | 73 to 79 |
| 100 to 106 | 97 to 103 | 94 to 100 | 91 to 97 | 94 to 100 | 91 to 97 | 88 to 94 | 85 to 91 | 88 to 94 | 85 to 91 | 82 to 88 | 79 to 85 | 2412<br>2314<br>2215<br>2117<br>2216<br>3-49<br>400<br>410 | S<br>S,75<br>S,75<br>S,75<br>S,75<br>A/C/C<br>Evln<br>Rdln | 222 A<br>245 A<br>245 C<br>276 B<br>276 A<br>203<br>219<br>181 | 2413<br>2314<br>2315<br>2216<br>2219<br>3-49<br>400<br>410 | S,75<br>S,75<br>S,75<br>S,75<br>S,75<br>A/C/C<br>Evln<br>Rdln | 250 A<br>256 B<br>280 A<br>288 B<br>330 A<br>212<br>228<br>189 | 2512<br>2413<br>2315<br>2415<br>2219<br>3-60<br>340<br>360 | S<br>S,75<br>S,75<br>S<br>S,75<br>A/C/C<br>Evln<br>Rdln | 257 A<br>260 B<br>292 B<br>306 A<br>344 B<br>226<br>258<br>209 | 2512<br>2315<br>2415<br>2219<br>3-60<br>340<br>360 | S<br>S,75<br>S<br>S,75<br>A/C/C<br>Evln<br>Rdln | 267 A<br>303 B<br>319 A<br>358 B<br>246<br>268<br>217 | 2512<br>2514<br>2317<br>3-71<br>300 | S<br>S,75<br>S,75<br>A/C/C<br>Evln | 277 B<br>306 A<br>358 A<br>268<br>294 | 2514<br>2613<br>2317<br>2419<br>3-71<br>300 | S,75<br>S<br>S,75<br>75<br>A/C/C<br>Evln | 317 B<br>322 A<br>371 B<br>407 A<br>278<br>305 | 2514<br>2613<br>2317<br>2419<br>3-71<br>300 | S,75<br>S<br>S,75<br>75<br>A/C/C<br>Evln | 329 B<br>333 A<br>365 B<br>422 A<br>298<br>316 | 2613<br>2419 | S<br>75 | 345 A<br>437 B | 2613 | S | 366 | | | | | | | 88 to 94 | 85 to 91 | 82 to 88 | 79 to 85 |

WARNING: Overstressing compound bows by using arrows lighter than AMO recommendations may cause damage to the bow and possible injury to the shooter.

AMO compound bow manufacturers have issued the following warning: "The total arrow weight (shaft weight shown in Easton chart plus weight of point, insert [if used] and fletching plus nock and UNI Bushing) should be greater than 6 grains per pound of peak bow weight for a 60# compound bow with a 30" draw length.*"

- Bow weights lighter than 60# and draw lengths shorter than 30" can use arrows lighter than 6 grains/pound of peak bow weight*.
- Bow weights heavier than 60# and draw lengths longer than 30" should use arrows heavier than 6 grains/pound of peak bow weight.*"

* For exact weights check "AMO Guidelines" in the Easton Tuning and Maintenance Guide.

# BEMAN HUNTING AND TARGET SHAFT LENGTH SELECTION CHART

ICSH = ICS Hunter
ICSF/Hawk = ICS Field/ICS Hawk
ICSCH = ICS Camo Hunter
Matrix = Carbonmetal Matrix

**Special Precautions for Carbon Shafts:**
Carbon arrows may be used for hunting if special precautions are taken. See your dealer or the information packaged with Beman carbon arrows and shafts.
Warning: Arrows must be carefully inspected before each shot to see that they have not been damaged.

They were also heavier and more expensive. Still, their better qualities won over many archers, particularly the hunters, some of whom still like them. And fiberglass arrows are acknowledged to be the best for bowfishing.

The innovation of tubular aluminum arrows came next. These quickly became the favorite of both target shooters and bowhunters, and they seem destined to remain so. It's logical, because aluminum shafts can be manufactured to extremely precise diameters, wall thicknesses or gauges, weight and stiffness to fit any condition or situation a shooter can encounter. This allows for more exact matching, and a greater variety of choices. There are other advantages. These arrows are moderately priced, and all but the most badly bent shafts can be put back into service with an inexpensive straightening device.

Carbon arrows have come on strong in recent years among both target shooters and hunters. They are lighter than aluminum shafts, allowing for greater arrow speed and flatter trajectory without a real sacrifice in energy. They are also stiffer; carbon arrows don't need to be straightened like aluminum arrows, making them more user-friendly for the average hunter.

Another popular new shaft is the aluminum/carbon composite (A/C/C), which has carbon fiber over an aluminum alloy core tube. This arrow combines some of the best features of both carbon and aluminum. While carbon

*Various kinds of fletching are available for different types of hunting and target shooting. These are a few examples of fletchings made with feathers, the standard material for centuries.*

*Fletching jigs like this one allow hunters interested in making their own arrows to glue all vanes on one shaft at the same time.*

and carbon composite shafts are a little more expensive than aluminum shafts, they will likely continue to grow in popularity, particularly as further improvements in arrow speed allow for lighter and lighter shafts.

## FLETCHING

Fletching is the arrow's guidance system, providing it with drag to maintain stability and rotation to keep it on course. Without fletching, the arrow is like a ship without a rudder, even though the shaft itself may be straight and true.

Throughout previous centuries and on into the present one, feathers have been the standard fletching material. They still occupy a major place, although the alternative of plastic vanes has become extremely popular among both target archers and bowhunters—particularly those using compound bows. The centershot handles don't require the flexibility of feathers, since the fletching doesn't touch as the arrow is shot. From the hunter's standpoint, plastic vanes are more durable and less noisy than feathers. Too, they perform well

*An arrow saw will cut shafts to precise lengths.*

in all kinds of weather conditions. This is especially important to hunters, because feathers can flatten when wet, rendering the arrow either useless or highly unpredictable in flight.

Because of the heavier shaft and broadhead, fletching on hunting arrows must be longer in order to provide stability. Plastic fletching is heavier than feathers, but the weight difference is small. Feather-fletched arrows leave the bow faster than ones with plastic, but they also slow down more rapidly. Ultimately it's a sort of tradeoff, and shooters can decide for themselves.

Whatever the material, fletching not only stabilizes the arrow, but it also determines how fast and how far it will travel, and several factors are involved when it comes to the purpose or result that's desired. If long range is the goal, one type will be best. If speed is the objective, there's a different formula. And let's not overlook the important aspect of plain old cosmetics. When it comes to that, it's hard to beat the kind of effects that can be created with bright-colored and barred or spotted feathers. Or natural-colored ones, for that matter.

Straight fletching was once the rule, but today shooters have a variety of configurations from which to choose—standard, left- and right-wing helical (spiral), and straight offset. The type chosen by individual shooters is really a matter of preference, since tests have shown that there's very little difference in the flight characteristics of the various kinds. The length of the fletching depends upon arrow length and weight and type of point used.

There are what can be called "specialty arrows" designed for specific purposes. Flu-flu fletching, for example, causes an arrow to have very limited range and a rapid loss of speed in flight. There are a number of different styles, but all are virtual balls of feathers at the terminal end of the shaft. Flu-flu arrows are used principally for wingshooting birds.

There are also arrows fletched specifically for bowfishing and frog hunting which have either plastic or rubber vanes.

Most shooters prefer arrows with three vanes, with one feather or vane set on the shaft at right angles to the slot of the nock. This is referred to as the "cock feather," and is often of a different color. The others are called "hen feathers" or "vanes." The use of four vanes isn't uncommon, and by comparison, the performance is about the same. However, in the excitement of hunting situations it's easy to incorrectly nock four-vane arrows, and perhaps the single disadvantage is enough to tip the scales in favor of the three-vane kind.

## MAKING YOUR OWN ARROWS

As shooters gain experience many start making their own arrows. The components for this kind of endeavor are easily obtainable. The major aluminum arrow maker offers a selection of blanks for every target or hunting need, and there is a kaleidoscopic array of fletching material to choose from, as well as different styles of nocks. Tools for every aspect of home arrow manufacture are sold, including fletching jigs, nock locators, alignment devices, straighteners, scales and other accessories. It's truly high-tech compared to the old days when almost everything was done from scratch!

Economy plays a part in this, but it isn't the key factor. Archers, particularly those who use traditional equipment, find great pleasure in being personally involved in as many aspects of shooting as possible. They can customize the arrows to whatever degree they wish, and producing their own arrows adds another measure of pride and self-satisfaction.

## POINTS FOR PRACTICE AND SMALL GAME

The type of activity in which an archer is going to be involved determines what kind of point or head will be used on the arrows, and there are ones designed for every target and bowhunting purpose.

Beginning shooters will generally start with field points with some form of blunt and graduate to other types as their skills increase. In the past, when wood or fiberglass arrows were used, points had to be affixed to the shaft with glue. With the development of tubular aluminum shafts, an insert placed in the end of the arrow allows the shooter to choose the kind of point needed for the activity involved. This makes it possible to purchase a set of arrows at the start and continue to shoot with them in many kinds of target or field situations as long as the proper balance is maintained.

Blunt points are not only for practice, but they're also useful for hunting small game where shock rather than penetration is all that's required. There are several varieties available.

Field points are used in practice, also, and they are intended to simulate both the weight and the flight characteristics of hunting arrows. This same kind of point is sometimes used for target shooting, but there are special target points that provide less weight and a greater degree of accuracy. Their design makes them easier to remove from targets, also.

*This broadhead system allows hunters to choose from dozens of blade configurations to meet different hunting situations.*

There are specialty points made for bowfishing. Some are much like harpoons in design, and others—called judo points or "grabbers," with wire arms of various dimensions—are very practical for use on small game and birds, and they also help stop arrows short and keep them from being lost under leaves and undergrowth.

## BROADHEADS FOR BOWHUNTING BIG GAME

The selection of broadheads available these days is extensive, with dozens of designs and configurations available. New versions pop up regularly in an already broadhead-inundated market. Exactly which broadhead you should choose will be influenced by a variety of factors, such as the distance you typically shoot,

*Replaceable-blade broadheads are very popular among hunters, as they require no sharpening. Dull blades can just be replaced with new, razor-sharp blades.*

*Expandable broadheads are a good match for hunters shooting light, fast arrows, although many hunters feel more comfortable shooting traditional fixed-blade broadheads when pursuing large game animals.*

the type of animals you pursue, and the arrow speed and kinetic energy you generate. Confidence in your choice can play a large role in your shooting.

The earliest broadhead models were relatively simple: solid, one-piece heads with two blades that required occasional sharpening. Next came broadheads with three blades, and shortly afterward heads with three or four pre-sharpened, removable blades that could be either replaced if damaged or resharpened and used again. There were also innovations such as blades with cutouts or vents that help improve accuracy; points with retractable blades that open up after penetration; heads with corkscrew or serrated blades and among these, blades so badly designed that they had poor flight capabilities. Some broadheads have cutting edges all the way to the tip and others have blades set back from the nose cone.

Today, there are three basic types of broadheads that hunters can choose from: replaceable blades, fixed blades, and mechanicals. Replaceable blades have become the most commonly used, as they are easily installed and require no sharpening. Once dulled, the blades are simply replaced with inexpensive new blades from the manufacturer that are razor sharp. One big advantage of this type of broadhead is that you can practice with the arrows with which you will be hunting and then just change the blades before heading afield, allowing a new level of confidence that your arrows will fly as they should. These blades have become just as reliable as fixed-blade broadheads. Tips are usually either cutting tips or chisel points. Cutting tips, tips with the blade running right to the end, are traditionally thought to penetrate better than chisel points—whose blades are set behind a nose cone with chiseled edges—because they start cutting immediately and create a bigger entry hole on impact. With most hunters shooting lighter arrows at higher speeds these days, this distinction may not be as important as it once was.

Mechanical heads are also becoming more popular as arrow speeds increase and arrow weights decrease. They offer more stable flights with less wind planing than regular broadheads, which often catch air as they move, decreasing accuracy, particularly in varied hunting conditions. The streamlined design of modern mechanicals reduces this problem. Mechanicals usually feature two or three blades connected to a ferrule. Upon impact, the blades open and fold back, locking in place to act just like fixed-blade broadheads. It is important to remember that mechanicals work best at higher arrow speeds, where impact ensures that the blades will expand and lock properly. Many traditional archers are still getting comfortable with expanding blades and their reliability. Mechanicals usually create a smaller entry wound, and there can be an increased chance of arrow deflection in certain situations as a shaft moves through an animal. But as the trend toward higher speed continues, hunters shooting lighter arrows will continue to look to mechanicals for better accuracy.

Fixed-blade heads have been around the longest of the three. They usually include two, three, or four blades. These broadheads tend to be a bit heavier, although many hunters feel better using them, as they are thought to create a larger hole with deeper penetration—particularly with the shorter distances over which hunting shots typically occur. The time and skill required to correctly sharpen fixed blades has turned off many hunters who prefer the low maintenance of replaceable blades and mechanicals. Many bowyers, though, prefer to sharpen their own broadheads. It is satisfying, but it also gives them additional confidence in this vital piece of equipment and makes a clean kill on big game even more meaningful. There are many sharpening tools available, some designed specifically for broadheads.

So, how do you select the best broadhead for your own use? This is something that requires an intelligent and prudent approach. Conscientious hunters don't experiment on game in the field; rather, they practice with life-size, three-dimensional targets that are made of material that closely approximates animal flesh in terms of density and resistance. Seeking the advice of other big-game bowhunters can help, also, since you can use their experiences to narrow the field of choices. Finally, when you find a broadhead that works well for you, stick with it. No matter how highly touted new versions may be, resist the temptation to switch until you learn more about them. Remember you're dealing with living creatures, and there is no excuse for reckless "testing" in the field. Factor in arrow speed, weight, the shooting distance in your average hunting situation, and penetration for the animals you usually hunt, then practice enough to get comfortable with a particular type of broadhead to feel confident of a quick, clean kill.

## MATCHING TO DRAW LENGTH

There are do-it-yourself methods of matching arrows to draw length, but visiting an archery pro shop to accomplish this and the other aspects of getting prepared is the most reliable way to get a satisfactory result.

For one thing, the standard formula for making this determination with longbows and recurve bows doesn't work with compound bows. The bow weight on the traditional bows has been marked on the basis of a 28-inch draw length, and while this works as a general rule, it isn't always accurate. Another method for making this determination is to measure an individual's arm spread and match it with a chart that indicates the length of arrow to be used. This formula covers differences in arm spread from 57 to 77 inches, and arrow lengths from 22 to 32 inches. Like other "formula" methods, this isn't a dependable technique. Even what seems to be the simplest of them all—drawing a long blank arrow in a lightweight bow to the anchor point and having someone mark the spot where the arrow crosses the leading edge of the bow—can't be trusted.

When it comes to compound bows, there are no established rules of thumb or formulas, because the draw length varies due to many factors, some related to the individual and others to the particular equipment being used.

Again, ask for professional help, at least in the beginning.

*Some hunters still prefer tabs or shooting gloves despite the fact that most archers now use some type of mechanical release.*

## BASIC ACCESSORIES

Beginning archers will get their basic training on targets, and even if this will occur on a range, it can be helpful to have a backyard target for additional practice.

Initially, the bullseye-type targets are the best for the beginner. They provide a specific spot for the eye to concentrate on, and this is the type used at most training facilities. For alternate practice away from the range, there's an inexpensive model mounted on a stand which has a series of flip-over targets that feature the standard bullseye and a variety of birds and animals. The latter selection is appealing to those archers who want to hunt game eventually. Several steps up from these flip-over targets are life-size, three-dimensional targets that are as close to the real thing as a shooter can find, even in terms of the density of the material used in the forms.

Wherever targets are set up, special attention should be paid to what's behind them so that arrows that pass through or miss can't do any harm. A good backstop usually will handle this best, but if you're shooting in an open

*Most mechanical releases are activated with tension on a trigger, but the Cascade Release goes off when you relax, letting pressure off the trigger.*

field, make sure there's nothing beyond the target within maximum arrow range that might be hit.

Arm guards worn on the inside of the forearm that holds the bow are essential in any shooting situation with any kind of bow, since they not only prevent painful abrasions from the bowstring, but also keep loose sleeves out of

*String silencers are available in many types of material, including the soft fleece shown here.*

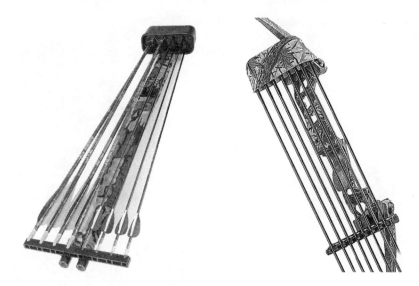

One- and two-piece quivers that attach to the bow are popular with hunters.

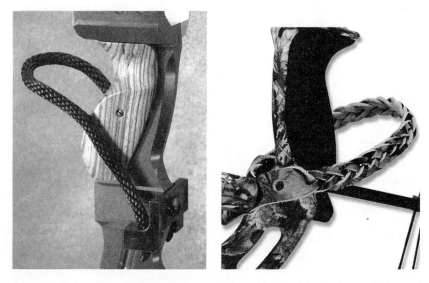

A wrist strap increases stability and ensures that the bow won't be inadvertently dropped at the shot.

*Bow slings let hunters keep their hands free when not shooting.*

the way. There are many versions of arm guards available, most of which are quite inexpensive. And until you get clothes designed for shooting, a chest guard is a device that's worth having.

No matter whether you use a traditional or a compound bow, you should include either a shooting glove or a tab as a necessary accessory. Both protect the fingers on the drawing hand and help assure a cleaner release.

Finger shooting was formerly the preferred method for teaching beginners, but the development of mechanical releases brought them into the forefront for both target shooters and bowhunters. There's wide diversity in the design and function of the mechanical releases, and it requires experimenting with many types to find the most suitable one with which to begin.

A quiver is another basic accessory, and even though a beginning shooter may be using only arrows with practice points, it's important that they be kept enclosed in a quiver at all times. Target shooters usually wear holster-type quivers that attach to the belt or around the waist, or the kind that fits over the shoulder on a strap. Field shooters or bowhunters usually have quivers that are attached to the bow with clips that hold the arrows firmly in place, and with hoods to cover points and fletching.

## OTHER ACCESSORIES

A good bow case is an important accessory, because it protects equipment that is being transported or stored. Soft cases with padding are suitable for local events or trips into the field when the equipment is under your personal supervision. Hard cases are best when equipment is being shipped, because they offer more protection. Also, some of the larger aluminum or plastic models are large enough to hold a lot more than just the basic tackle, including extra parts and even clothing items.

Those using longbows or recurve bows should have a good cord bowstringer (to aid in safe and easy stringing and to keep from damaging the bow), a stringkeeper (to maintain the proper brace height of the string and protect the lower limb tip when the bow is unstrung), and a bow square. According to the type of equipment, having a few other items along is helpful: extra nocking points, bowstrings, a small repair kit. As your skills progress and you begin to diversify, your accessory list will expand.

# EQUIPMENT AND INSTRUCTION FOR YOUNGSTERS

The compound bow has made getting into archery more attractive to youngsters because they can begin with tackle that can be used for practice on standard ranges instead of just backyard targets. Previously, a youth had to begin with a particular draw weight and bow length, which during the learn-

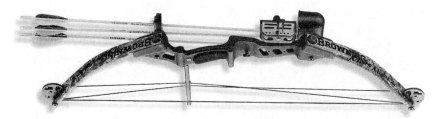

*Most bow manufacturers offer bows that adjust to grow with young archers.*

ing—and growing—process had to be periodically upgraded or altered. The compound bow's adjustable weight and let-off features permit an experienced shooter or pro shop specialist to start a youngster of practically any age with gear of professional caliber. There are mini-bows that perform remarkably well, yet which even small children can draw easily.

Just as important as equipment selection is the next step, which is thorough and competent instruction in the fundamentals of shooting and all of the vital safety factors. Most archery clubs welcome young shooters to participate and provide assistance and encouragement. Also, the majority of states throughout the nation have hunter safety courses administered by the game and fish agencies. Successful completion of the course is a requirement for obtaining a hunting license. There is also an excellent manual produced by the National Bowhunter Education Foundation which contains a wealth of information from the basics of the sport to the preparation of game for the table. The NBEF address is listed in Appendix A.

All of the training shouldn't be left up to clubs or agencies. Parents or friends can supervise beginners, and in the case of children, should keep a close eye on them at all times when they have archery equipment in their hands. It's easy for youngsters to get a little irresponsible and shoot at things other than the target, or shoot arrows into the air to see how far they will fly. They must come down, of course, and a descending arrow can inflict serious injury or damage property. Shooting at a lower angle into an open field is a better idea. And just as with firearms, the cardinal rule applies: "Never aim at anything you don't intend to shoot!"

Rules of safety must be constantly kept in mind, not only in regard to your own conduct but in awareness of what others are doing, like driving in a car defensively. Being confident of your own ability doesn't make you immune from becoming a casualty.

# 2

# LEARNING TO SHOOT

It's necessary to learn the fundamentals of the bow and its function before actually attempting to start shooting. Some of the steps relating to this are required only with the longbow and recurve bow, but they are important for these kinds of equipment.

## BRACING THE BOW

There are a variety of methods of stringing bows safely and properly. For example, there is a wood device that works well for backyard shooting or indoor and outdoor ranges. It's not handy to carry around, though, so the pocket-size cord stringer is much more widely used. This is a length of nylon cord with leather pockets at each end. You place one pocket on the lower nock and slip the other over the opposite end, then stand on it and pull up at the handle. This creates the necessary curve that allows the upper bowstring to be slipped into place. This technique works for both longbows and recurves.

To string by hand, use what's known as the "step-across" method. Frankly, you're well advised to have it explained and demonstrated by a profi-

*No one will shoot well consistently without good form and regular practice.*

cient archer than to try to do it yourself by following written instructions. The late Fred Bear described this procedure many years ago, and his instructions prove this point:

"First, the string loop should be in place on the lower bow nock and held in place by a rubber band or bow tip protector. Holding the other string loop in the left hand, step across the bow with the right leg so that the bow handle lies against the back of the thigh as high up as possible. Your right leg is between the bow and the bowstring. The pressure of the thigh must be against the bow handle to avoid bending one limb more than the other. Hold the upper bow limb just under the recurve in your right hand and place the lower recurve over the instep of your left foot, being careful not to let the bow tip touch the floor or ground. (Some archers use a leather harness slipped on over the shoe to hold the bow tip in the right position.) Now apply pressure backward with your thigh on the bow by leaning forward from the waist and applying pressure with the right hand. The string loop held in the left hand can then be slipped into place in the upper nock. Before releasing pressure, make sure the string loops are firmly seated in the bow nocks."

This isn't all, but it's enough to boggle any beginner's mind and inspire gratitude for compound bows. And to give credit where it's due, Fred Bear's final comment on the subject was that it is best to get a bowstringing device.

## BRACE HEIGHT

For longbows, this refers to the distance between the bow handle and the string. Normally this was about 6 inches. The brace height of modern bows is measured at right angles with a bow square from the string to the deepest cut on the handle. Because of the variety of handle designs and configurations on today's bows, the brace height is usually recommended by the manufacturer, and the commercially made bowstrings they supply with each bow will ordinarily provide the right brace height or be very close to it. The correct height keeps noise, vibration and wrist slap to a minimum and influences arrow flight. New bowstrings will stretch, but when they reach their final length, the proper height can be adjusted by twisting the string a few turns in the direction that tightens the serving, the bound portions of the string in the center and at the ends.

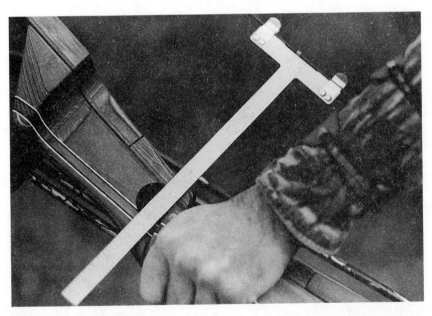

*A bow square is useful in determining the nocking point and brace height on a traditional bow and making adjustments on compound bows.*

For compound bows, each manufacturer has a recommended brace height for each model. This can be increased or decreased by turning the limb bolts to change the angle, or "tiller," of the limbs.

## NOCKING POINT

The nocking point on a bowstring is an indicator that ensures correct placement of the arrow, and there are various ways archers mark its position. The simplest is a few wraps of thread coated with cement, but just as easy to install are the metal slip-on or heat-shrink type.

A bow square is the best tool for quickly determining the exact place for the nocking point. It should be ⅛ to ¾₆ inch above the arrow rest. Once in place, the nocking point indicates exactly where the nock of the arrow should be placed. When nocked, the arrow can look peculiar because of the downward angle. But this is the best alignment for smoothly launching the arrow.

Differences in shooting styles and whether or not the shooter uses a mechanical release or fingers will determine the exact nock placement.

*Slip-on nocks can be easily installed in proper position with nocking pliers.*

# SIX STEPS TO SHOOTING SKILL

Shooting skills can be accomplished only by following the six commandments basic to the learning process: Standing, Nocking, Drawing, Holding and Aiming, Releasing, and Follow-through. Practice each step of the program until you have mastered it.

## STANCE

You can establish a comfortable stance without equipment in hand. The feet should be placed apart far enough for good balance, with the toes approximately at a 90-degree angle to the target. Some shooters come to prefer a precise square stance, while others find they shoot better with an open stance. The latter positions the body so that there is less chance of the bowstring colliding with the chest or forearm.

With your head erect, turn it toward the target, and hold it steady. After doing this a few times, you can quite naturally assume the proper stance, at which time you add the bow and begin the additional sequences of instruction and practice.

*Take a balanced, comfortable stance before the draw.*

By the time you first bring the bow into the picture, chances are that you'll have tried it out at the pro shop and handled it enough so that it feels comfortable in your hand. Don't grip the handle; instead, let it lie easily in the V between the thumb and forefinger. The pressure when drawing must come at this point, not at the heel or palm of the hand, and it's vital that the wrist is held straight and not bent, and that the handle *never* be gripped hard. This would create improper alignment and cause the string to strike the forearm or wrist. It would also seriously reduce accuracy.

## NOCKING

The bow should be held in a horizontal position while the arrow is nocked by grasping the arrow between thumb and forefinger with the cock feather or vane up. The nock should be slid into position snugly against the nocking point. For a finger release, hook the first three fingers of the hand over the string with the arrow between the first and second fingers. A glove should always be worn for protection. With a mechanical release, the procedure is different.

## DRAWING

The draw is where many beginning shooters experience their most nagging problems, because it involves some of the most critical aspects of shooting. Once the bow is raised to a vertical position the draw should be a smooth, uninterrupted movement that includes pushing forward with the arm that holds the bow and pulling back with the hand that controls the string until it reaches the side of the face. The drawing arm should be held on a level with the shoulder so it is in line with the arrow at full draw.

The shoulder muscles provide most of the power for the draw. Since some of these muscles are not normally used, the draw weight may at first seem a little too great, but as the muscles tone up and become conditioned it will begin to feel comfortable. A bit of patience is required, but this is true of any learning procedure.

Some of the problems encountered by beginners in the past, such as arrows falling off just before release, have been eliminated with the development of new kinds of arrow rests and other equipment advancements. The compound bow and mechanical releases have been the most significant in this respect.

One of the most important aspects of the draw is that it allows an anchor point to be determined. This is the point to which the index or middle finger is brought on the draw. Experiment with this until you find the one that feels most natural and comfortable. Once you have established this, use it consistently. Be aware, though, that different shooting methods may require that you vary the anchor point; nevertheless, this isn't always the case.

## HOLDING AND AIMING

The slight pause, or hold, that occurs at the completion of the draw in order to aim has been given extended life, so to speak, by the let-off system of the compound bow. With longbows or recurve bows, the maximum draw weight is being felt at this moment, so there's a quite limited amount of time the position can be maintained. Not only that, but with these bows additional pressure must be applied during the pause. Otherwise, the arrow will creep forward, adversely affecting its flight and accuracy.

*Holding and aiming are much easier with a compound bow because the let-off system reduces the weight being drawn.*

*Establishing an anchor point will ensure consistent arrow flight.*

It's important that the target be the focus of attention when aiming, because if everything else is in order, where the arrow is going to strike is the major concern. It's good to practice concentrating on the target and getting the feel of the equipment, because no matter what kind of bow you're using, this helps to develop an instinct for the entire process. Once this is accomplished, most archers can actually shoot reasonably well with only the most basic equipment.

## RELEASE AND FOLLOW-THROUGH

Mechanical releases have been gaining in popularity, and justifiably so. For one thing, the finger release creates slightly more torque than a mechanical release and sometimes makes more noise. Too, mechanical releases are easier to use. Yet whatever method is used, the moment of release is extremely critical both in competition and in hunting. With all else in place, a clean, crisp release is what can assure that the arrow will fly truly and properly.

*It is important to stay in position until the arrow hits the target.*

The next second (or part of a second) after release—the follow-through—has to be classed as just as vital. Failing to perform this properly can spoil all previous efforts.

Follow-through involves keeping the bow arm perfectly still and rigid as the arrow is released and as it goes on its way to the target. Any movement at the moment the arrow is launched will affect its flight, so the best rule is to remain statue-like until it strikes the mark. Follow-through is also essential to good performance in golf, skeet shooting and tennis. The difference is that in those sports players have to continue a motion rather than hold in place.

## AIMING AIDS

Archers who either use traditional bows by choice or compete on ranges in the classes that ban any kind of aiming aids still use some of the techniques once considered as standard shooting practices. All of these are effective, but a beginner is much better served by using a bowsight, which will help produce satisfactory results more quickly. One reason a sight seems natural is because

*Practicing your shooting in a variety of positions that simulate situations you might encounter in the field will boost confidence.*

*Hunters using a finger release ordinarily employ a grip on the string with one finger over the nock and two fingers under.*

most people have already shot or pointed a gun when they first pick up a bow and are accustomed to using a sight.

Before the invention of the bowsight, the various methods prescribed for learning to aim were primarily point-of-aim, instinctive, gap shooting, three fingers under and string walking. Each requires guesswork to a large degree, from the standpoint of either distance to the target or the trajectory the arrow will follow. Also, by comparison with learning with a bowsight, these procedures are cumbersome and often extremely confusing.

Point-of-aim required the archer to aim over the point of the arrow at a spot between the shooter and the target and not look up at the target until after the arrow was released. It's a method that can be considered obsolete.

Instinctive shooting is still practiced, but it's definitely a kind of skill not every archer has the ability to master. This method requires an archer to aim and shoot automatically, and many people don't possess this ability. It's much like picking up a stone and hurling it at an object without any consideration of distance, size or its speed in motion. Those who can perform in this way are

---

**LEARNING TO HIT YOUR TARGET**
By Harold Knight
*Cadiz, Kentucky*

One of the main things to learn in hitting your target is how to judge distance, and one of the best ways to learn is simply by practicing while you're out scouting or hunting. For example, first estimate the distance, then actually step it off. You'll soon become quite adept at judging distance. There is no good substitute for practice.

It's important to shoot bow equipment that you can handle. Don't make the mistake, as many people do, of overweighting your bow. I prefer the equipment of today over the kind I used when I began to hunt 35 years ago. Back then, the arrows were made of wood and feathers, and a great deal of time was spent sharpening the broadhead. Also, it was not unusual to have to go through 50 shafts before finding 6 straight ones. Today the broadhead is presharpened to a razor edge for a good, clean, quick kill.

The sight system introduced on bows has been a tremendous help in hitting the target. It gives the ability to select a specific part of the animal instead of simply aiming at the entire animal and hoping you'll hit a critical area.

Another welcome improvement in recent years is in the area of tree stands. They are more comfortable and safer, enabling one to stay in the tree longer while hunting. Clothing also has improved; it's much warmer and drier.

Bowhunting has always been a favorite sport of mine. I like the challenge it offers. I think one of the most difficult things to do in North America is to harvest a whitetail trophy buck with bow and arrow!

*Harold Knight is a consummate outdoorsman who is thoroughly versed in all aspects of woods lore. With this background, it is natural that he is the inventor of many game calls, including the Tube Turkey Call and the Double-Grunt Deer Call. They are manufactured by his company, Knight/Hale Game Calls. Harold conducts many seminars throughout the U.S. on various aspects of hunting, and hunting deer and elk with a bow is at the very top of his preference list.*

---

fortunate, and it can be greatly satisfying to bowhunters who are able to instantly let an arrow fly and feel confident of hitting the target. However, it's a skill that isn't suitable for tournament shooting.

Gap shooting is closely linked to instinctive shooting, because with this method the shooter concentrates strictly on the target, yet remains conscious of the distance so that the point of the arrow can be adjusted accordingly. In rifle shooting, gap shooting would be classed as a form of "Kentucky windage" that requires guesswork based on a lot of experience.

Both three fingers under and string walking are ways to bring the arrow closer to the eye. With three fingers under, the anchor point is often moved from the corner of the mouth to the cheekbone to get a sort of down-the-gun-barrel view of the arrow, which is especially useful when aiming at close ranges. In string walking, the drawing fingers move farther down the string. The lower the fingers, the closer the arrow is to the eye.

Many traditional archers continue to use these methods, and even though most of today's beginners learn with a compound bow equipped with a sight, almost all eventually experiment with other kinds of equipment and shooting methods. This can add pleasure and a better appreciation of the sport. Also, discovering one has a talent for instinctive shooting, or the ability to learn it, can be quite a confidence booster.

## KINDS OF SIGHTS

A beginner's bowsight can be as basic as a single pin that is backed up with a bowstring peep sight, enabling easier alignment with the target. With a pin properly placed for a particular yardage, the shooter learns how to achieve dependable accuracy. It's then a simple matter to use multiple pins set for different distances and arrow variations.

Many types of bowsights are available. They range from the conventional to the exotic in both design and function. Some bowsights have multiple pins or a single moveable pin. Others have a crosshair system, and still others have fiber optic pins for low light conditions. There are pendulum sights for

*Pin sights (left) and scope sights (right) often incorporate fiber optic pins for low-light conditions.*

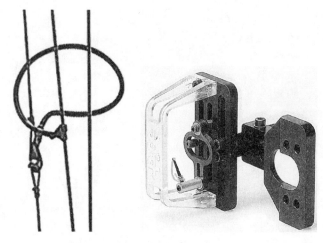

*Peep sights (left) remain popular with many archers. There are also sights developed specifically for shooting from tree stands (right) that adjust for range and angle.*

use in tree stands, basic telescopic sights, and scopes with laser-like lighted dots. And there are many more.

## IMPROVING YOUR AIM

The next step in preparing for hitting live targets is to use various tactics for improving your aim at different distances.

Pick a comfortable range and keep working at the target until you can consistently place a group of arrows within 2 or 3 inches. Stay with that range until it feels natural to you, then move back about 5 yards and work at that distance. Keep increasing your distance from the target 5 yards at a time until you are getting tight groups of arrows from about 40 yards, then begin varying your distance from session to session to retain control at all ranges.

At each range, practice shooting from various positions: standing, kneeling, sitting, leaning around a bush or even lying prone on the ground. Try different angles, such as high shots from stands or a ladder.

Practice in different lighting conditions such as you would encounter in the field. The more you duplicate field conditions and become familiar with them, the better you will be prepared for your first venture into the field. More advanced types of practice include various games, which are described in Chapter 14.

# 3

# WHEN THINGS GO WRONG

A ll archers encounter problems of one sort or another as time passes, some caused by human error and others by either faulty or mismatched equipment. The main thing is to recognize that something is wrong and to correct it as quickly as possible. The longer you allow a problem to linger, the more detrimental the effect can be on your shooting ability, confidence and progress as a shooter.

The initial step is determining what's causing the difficulty—for example, inaccurate arrow flight. The best way to determine what's causing this is to have an experienced archer watch you shoot, because chances are that the culprit is you rather than your equipment.

Bad habits that are sometimes unnoticed by the unsupervised shooter are easy to develop, but they will sooner or later begin to affect accuracy and consistency. Yet they're very easy to see by a qualified person looking over your shoulder. Erratic arrow flight is almost always due to errors in stance, draw, aiming, release or something similar, and once spotted, usually only small adjustments are needed to get things back on track.

If the problem is in the equipment, it's often easy to spot. Examine your arrows carefully for damage, and check for cracked or broken nocks. A cracked or misaligned nock can cause erratic and even dangerous arrow flight or a "dry-fire"—where the arrow separates from the bowstring before release (essentially, as if there had been no arrow in place)—which can harm the bow.

If there seems to be no problem with the arrow, it's best to have the bow checked out by professionals to be sure all of the components are matched and balanced. Regardless of where it was purchased, the best move is to take it to a pro shop where the trouble can be expertly diagnosed. If the equipment isn't functioning properly, manufacturers are usually happy to replace it at no cost and offer any additional assistance they can in making sure everything gets back in proper order.

## SAFETY IN THE FIELD

Safety on the range and in the field is of paramount importance, and even though accidents will occur no matter how careful the shooter may be, paying particular attention to likely causes can reduce their incidence.

This responsibility begins with the basics—equipment—because without proper care, maintenance and handling these items provide potential danger. Consider a few of them:

- Bowstrings that are too heavy, too light, frayed or weak can cause an array of problems: equipment damage, injury to the shooter, or erratic arrow flight.
- Arrows, especially razor-sharp broadheads, are hazardous when in flight, of course, but they can just as easily inflict injury or cause death through carelessness or mishandling. As such, arrows should be regularly inspected for flaws in fletching and straightness. All arrows should be carried in a quiver, but those with broadheads should be contained in the kind that has a hard shield covering the points.
- When hunting from an elevated stand, the hunter should always leave the shooting equipment on the ground and, only after getting in place, pull it up. Also, be sure to lower it *before* you descend.

*A harness should always be worn when hunting from a tree stand.*

- *Always* use a safety belt when ascending a tree, and keep it on all of the time you are in the stand.
- Make certain to inform a companion with you in the field or someone at home where you're going to be hunting. That way, if something goes wrong and you're injured or incapacitated, they'll know where to look for you.
- Bowhunters must follow the same primary rules of safety they learned in target or range shooting, but there are additional elements to be considered. Shooters must be certain that there is a clear path between their positions and where the target is likely to be. If this isn't the case, one must simply refrain from releasing an arrow.
- Most vital is that the hunter be *absolutely sure* of the target before shooting. One of the best pieces of advice ever given on this matter is in *Woodcraft*, a book written in 1888 by a writer who used the pen name "Nessmuk." In it he said: "In still-hunting, swear yourself black in the face never to shoot at a dim, moving object in the woods for a

deer, unless you have seen that it is a deer. In these days there are quite as many hunters as deer in the woods; and it is a heavy, wearisome job to pack a dead or wounded man ten or twelve miles out to a clearing, let alone that it spoils all the pleasure of the hunt and it apt to raise hard feelings among his relations."

Anticipate conditions that you may encounter in the field and be prepared for them. Having an emergency kit is wise, and a knowledge of how to give first aid treatment is essential.

Some of the items that should be considered for inclusion: first aid kit, ace bandage, canteen, trail food, waterproof match box, multi-bladed Swiss army knife or one of the sturdy folding devices that includes an array of tools, battery-powered strobe blinker, flashlight and extra batteries, extra midget flashlight, signal mirror, whistle, compass, or GPS device, map, emergency blanket, long-life candle, length of rope, plastic bags, a small roll of duct tape, water purification tablets and topo map of the area you're hunting.

You can add or delete from this list, but the main thing is to be sure the most vital elements are always included.

If you become lost or disoriented, stop and determine the direction you plan to take. Mark a spot with surveyor's tape or a strip of cloth, then keep repeating this at about 50-yard intervals. This can serve two purposes: First, it will give someone searching for you a trail to follow; and second, if you decide you've made the wrong choice you can easily backtrack, collecting the markers as you go to be used on your next attempt to solve the dilemma.

When you haven't found your way out, plan to make a signal fire (if you're in an area where fires are allowed). Smoke signals by day or a bright glow at night may bring rescuers to your site.

Weather can be a menace, particularly in the high country of the West where dramatic changes can occur very quickly. Go prepared for this kind of eventuality with what it takes to survive for several days.

You may find natural shelter from the elements under a rock overhang or other protective feature. Snow provides insulation, and a bed of dry brush or leaves in your shelter will help keep you warm on very cold nights.

One of the most common dangers encountered in the field is hypothermia. Its early stages have few warning signs, so when it strikes the effects are far advanced and can be lethal. Because of this, *precaution* is just as important as *treatment*.

**BACKCOUNTRY BOWHUNTING**
By Dwight Schuh
*Nampa, Idaho*

If one fact explains my bowhunting success, it's hunting undisturbed animals. They're less wary than heavily hunted game, and they follow normal daily patterns. To find these kinds of animals, I either hunt off-road as far as possible or seek out places no one else has thought to hunt. To find undisturbed pockets, I study maps, analyzing the country for roadless or rough terrain, blocks cut off by private land, or places so obvious they are overlooked by everyone else.

A daypack may be the most important backcountry hunting road. The pack eliminates fear and lets you hunt most efficiently. My pack has a lightweight frame and padded hip belt, which allows me to carry weight more comfortably than does a rucksack or fanny pack. In addition to hunting items—knife, game bags, and the like—my pack always contains topographic maps, compass, flashlight (with extra batteries and bulb), fire starter, emergency shelter, plastic flagging, first aid kit and warm jacket. With these items I feel comfortable to hunt anywhere, knowing that even if I get lost or hurt, I'll survive comfortably. That knowledge means efficient backcountry hunting.

The frame pack allows me to pack meat easily. I can load it with 70 or 80 pounds of meat on the spot and carry my game back to camp, without returning to camp for a "meat" frame. To retrieve animals from the backcountry, I bone them out and carry nothing but pure meat. I'd rather carry a deer on my back 5 miles than drag it 100 yards.

Even if I'm camping near a road, I go prepared to hunt off-road. In addition to my small frame pack, my gear always includes a lightweight sleeping bag, backpack stove and cookware, freeze-dried foods and lightweight shelter. Then if I discover some good animals more than a day's hike off-road, I can bivouac within easy hunting distance of the animals.

These tips help me to hunt undisturbed backcountry animals. I think they'll work for you, too.

*Dwight Schuh is bow and arrows editor for* Sports Afield *and as a freelance writer has been a contributor to all the major bowhunting magazines. He has been bowhunting for 20 years and considers backcountry bowhunting for deer and elk a specialty. Dwight has taken several Pope & Young record-book animals.*

Hypothermia results from what could be called a "deep chill" in which the temperature of the internal organs drops gradually by slow cooling. Frigid conditions can certainly be a cause, as one would logically suspect, yet people often succumb to hypothermia in temperatures as mild as 40 to 50 degrees when wind, wetness or a combination of both make it impossible for the body to ward off the chill.

Dressing properly is important, but this alone can't prevent falling into the water or being disabled in bad weather situations. That's why it's vital to carry survival equipment at all times. The "musts" for cool weather are fire-starting kits, an emergency blanket, a pocket-size emergency sleeping bag, and extra dry clothes. Other lifesavers can be a small stove or heat tabs and instant soup or other beverage. Getting something warm inside can be extremely helpful. And when you have these articles with you, it's often better to wait it out rather than to strike out on your own at the mercy of the elements.

When emergency situations involve accidents, a thoroughly prepared bowhunter will have the knowledge and training necessary to handle even serious ones. Many things that can (and do) happen in the field require more than just bandages and antibiotic creme.

Typical are the many falls hunters suffer while climbing trees, alone or with a stand, or from the stand itself once they are in position. Tumbling from a height of 15 or 20 feet can inflict a lot of physical damage, and it isn't uncommon to have broken bones, concussions and other injuries as a result.

You should also know how to treat bleeding and have actual practice in "pressure dressing" a wound. There are different treatments for chest wounds, abdominal injuries and bleeding from extremities. In case of injury, panic is an enemy. You will want to act quickly, but knowing exactly what to do and what not to do will give you confidence and help you to remain calm.

Knowing what to do can also mean the difference between life and death. Because of this, it can be extremely valuable to take an advanced first aid course that teaches the emergency setting of fractures, treatment of head injuries, CPR and other resuscitation procedures.

Nor is having this kind of training just for the benefit of the other person. There's always the possibility that someday you will find it advantageous to use the expertise on yourself. Nobody is excluded from the probability of accidents.

Thoughts of this sort make a good point for use of the "buddy system," because regardless of a person's knowledge of how to respond to emergencies, a lone individual can be incapacitated and unable to function.

The Boy Scout motto, "Be Prepared," is good to remember. Even better for bowhunters in the field, though, might be to insert one more word ("Well"), placed right in the middle!

# 4

# ETHICS

There is no way to overstate the importance of ethics in bowhunting. The acceptance or rejection of the sport in the eyes of the public, or in those of other hunters, is greatly affected by the kind of conduct and responsibility displayed by the participants.

Webster defines "ethics" as "the study of standards of conduct and moral judgment," deriving from Latin and Greek words referring to "character, custom." What is considered ethical, then, is what conforms to the actions deemed acceptable by a given group. To bring the question home, consider how the decisions each bowhunter personally makes and how the kind of behavior that results square with the prevailing "acceptable" standards. The buck stops with the individual.

It's no secret that bowhunters come under closer scrutiny than other members of the hunting community, and some of the reasons for this can be traced directly to a variety of unethical practices. It isn't a question of whether or not this scrutiny is warranted; the point is that everyone should make a special effort to help reduce the criticism and improve the sport's image.

Today virtually all bowhunting organizations place the ethics question high on their list of important issues. It is a subject given great emphasis in seminars conducted by organizations and by individuals, where the question is not only the individual's role but the overall image of bowhunting. Sometimes, an entire seminar is devoted to bowhunting ethics. Most experts consider these points to be imperative:

# WHAT TO DO

*Know Your Equipment:* This is a basic step in the area of personal responsibility, and it has to do with both the individual's safety as well as that of other hunters. It's necessary to be totally familiar with all of your equipment and hunting gear, certain that it's in good condition and fully functional, and confident in your ability to use it.

*Know Yourself:* Every hunter should be fully aware of his or her capabilities, and that means an honest self-evaluation to establish boundaries and make certain you don't exceed them. For instance, there's a big difference between shooting at a target range and drawing on a big buck. In a hunting situation the elements of excitement and anticipation can override skills and judgment. It's better to be too conservative in making decisions than too bold.

*Keep Practicing:* Bowhunters, like concert pianists, ballet dancers and high wire performers, can't maintain their level of proficiency without constant, year-round practice. Some sports don't require this kind of dedication, but bowhunting does. Most bowhunters enjoy practicing and look forward to it, so it's not regarded as a chore.

*Accuracy:* Clean, quick kills are the goal of every bowhunter. Achieving them requires both the ability to place arrows accurately and a thorough knowledge of the anatomy of the animal being hunted. The kill zones aren't the same, particularly in big-game species, so doing some homework on this subject is important. There are plenty of good references available in sporting goods stores and books on big-game hunting. What usually isn't included are the places to plant arrows when the animal is at angles other than broadside. This is where practice on 3-D targets can be very helpful.

*Follow-up:* The recovery of wounded game is a task all bowhunters should feel morally obligated to perform to the very best of their ability, regardless of the time or effort involved. Disregarding this responsibility and leaving

*Always be sure of your target before taking a shot in the field.*

a crippled animal to suffer or die is inexcusable. There are many ways to avoid losing wounded animals, including game trackers attached to the arrow, arrows equipped with sonic devices, infrared game finders, and chemicals that make blood trails more visible.

*Go by the Rules:*   All bowhunters should be fully knowledgeable of the current hunting rules and regulations in their home state or wherever else they may be afield. Breaking the law is a serious personal mistake, yet it also reflects on other participants in the sport. A few bad apples can have an enormous impact. Something else: bowhunters who care for the sport shouldn't be reluctant to report violations. It's their responsibility to do so if they wish to preserve the idea of good sportsmanship.

*Respect Landowners' Rights:*   No one has the privilege of trespassing on private land without permission, yet this is one of the most common examples of bad behavior displayed by hunters. Those who ignore "No Hunting" signs create ill will among property owners and cause more lands to be posted. Such actions also help generate more anti-hunting sentiment among the general public. Many states have laws that require a hunter to have the written consent of a landowner, and in most places this is strictly enforced. Basically, though, it comes down to the matter of hunter behavior.

*Respect for Others:* This is where application of the Golden Rule would be quite enough, because simple politeness is the main point. By nature, hunting is somewhat of a competitive sport, but this should be a contest between hunter and quarry, not hunter versus hunter. Don't intrude on other hunters' territory by setting up a stand nearer than 100 yards from their position, and if you are on the move give them a wide berth so as not to spook game that may be in the vicinity. Crowding results in the loss of opportunity for all parties. Also, you can win yourself a star by offering to assist a fellow bowhunter drag a big-game animal out of the woods.

*Know the Issues:* Bowhunters should make sure they're up to date on current problems and issues relating to the sport and are able to talk about them in an intelligent and calm manner to critics or other hunters. Knowledgeable hunters make favorable impressions and improve relations with others; ignorant or hot-headed individuals don't. It isn't difficult to become well informed and remain so, since there's a constant flow of information on these subjects in newspapers, magazines, and on television and radio.

*Boost the Sport:* All hunters share the spotlight of attention that's focused on them by the general public, and rather than shrink from it, they should use the opportunity to boost the sport. It must be remembered that all nonhunters aren't anti-hunters, and sometimes they're more curious than critical. Most laymen don't understand wildlife management and the need for balanced game populations. They also often aren't aware of the fact that hunters' dollars are what fund the conservation programs responsible for maintaining and perpetuating not only the species that are hunted but nongame species as well. The public needs to recognize that the majority of bowhunters are conscientious and proficient, and that the sport is wholesome and safe.

## WHAT NOT TO DO

Anyone with experience in the field is aware of the things that some hunters do—or fail to do—that are bad for bowhunting. They're all correctable by using a little common sense.

*Presenting a Negative Image:* The media sometimes depicts hunters as slobs, and those who go afield unshaven and dressed sloppily help to validate this caricature in the minds of many people. Viewing a hunting trip as relaxing is okay, but personal appearance shouldn't be neglected in the process of "unwinding." After all, you're almost certain to be seen, and neither the public nor other hunters will react favorably.

*Acting in an Offensive Manner:* Nothing damages the image of hunting more than those who drink in public and use loud and offensive language. Everyone knows that alcohol and lethal weapons don't mix, and this kind of behavior sends out far-reaching ripples of criticism that are impossible to counter. Nearly as harmful are hunters who boast of "sticking" animals and losing them, or who like to portray themselves and bowhunting as "macho" through their actions and the display of repulsive slogans on hats, bumper stickers and T-shirts.

*Bad Taste in Displaying Game:* At one time it was acceptable to drape a big-game kill over the hood of a car and triumphantly exhibit it on the trip home. That's no longer the case. The display of dead animals isn't appreciated by the public nor, for that matter, by most hunters. The same applies to photographs of harvested game. They can be posed in a tasteful and attractive manner without showing bullet wounds or open body cavities. Pride in a trophy is justified, but it should be demonstrated tactfully.

## COURTESY TOWARD LANDOWNERS

Bowhunting often takes place on lands owned by other individuals, or by corporations or government agencies. Being considerate of the property owner should be the aim of every hunter. Some simple rules of thumb are widely accepted, for obvious reasons.

First, be sure you have permission before you hunt on someone else's property, and find out what restrictions the owner requires. For example, building a permanent tree stand may not be allowed, or the owner may not be willing for you to start a campfire on the property.

Be careful not to damage trees or crops. Do not drive off-road without permission or block trails with your vehicle. It is a good idea to leave a sign on your vehicle showing your name, address and phone number.

Be sure to remove all evidence of your visit—the carcass and all organs, as well as any garbage that remains. Heavy trash bags are useful for this purpose. In fact, leave everything the way you found it.

Small, quiet groups work better than large, noisy ones when bowhunting. Silent drives with just a few hunters protect the environment for others who may want to hunt the same location the next day.

By showing consideration for the property owner, you are enhancing the perception of bowhunters as responsible people and creating a positive image not only for yourself but for your fellow hunters.

The popularity of the ethics question and its widespread discussion in seminars and training courses are having a significant effect. Virtually every new bowhunter has been indoctrinated in ethical behavior, and hunters violating these rules are coming under increasing pressure to change their ways. The impact of these education efforts will ultimately assure more conscientious bowhunters and a public that is better informed.

# 5

# BIG-GAME ANIMALS

The North American continent offers probably the greatest "menu" of big-game species of any region except Africa. At one time, nearly all of these species were sought exclusively with rifles, but during the past several decades, the bow has been gaining popularity as an alternate tool for taking large animals.

More than any other single factor, the resurgence of the whitetail deer in North America has been responsible for the phenomenal growth in the number of people who have become active big-game hunters. Some individuals have taken up the bow and arrow as their initial hunting venture; some added it as another skill they wished to master; and still others are hunters who abandoned the gun in favor of the challenges bowhunting offers.

What's also significant is that once the door was opened for bowhunters to seek these animals, the acceptance of the bow as a legitimate and suitable hunting tool for all types of big game spread like wildfire, not only throughout North America but to other parts of the world as well. Today, there's almost no large game animal species that can't be hunted with a bow anywhere on this continent, and that includes everything from the innocuous species to those that can—and will—literally eat you alive!

One word of caution: With all that's available, it's easy to "get too big for your britches," as the old saying goes, and tackle things beyond your capabilities. A wise bowhunter will progress in A-B-C manner when it comes to expanding his or her horizons, moving ahead only when sufficient experience and knowledge have been gained. That's the sensible and ethical way to go about it, and it pays off in terms of success and personal satisfaction.

But back to whitetails and the bonuses that bowhunters enjoy, which attract more participants every year. One of these is the increased amount of hunting opportunity the sport provides.

## WHITETAIL DEER

Whitetail deer are the most widely distributed big-game species in North America. They're found throughout southern Canada, throughout the forty-eight contiguous states except in the far Southwest, everywhere in Mexico ex-

*Whitetail deer*

cept the Baja Peninsula, and also in Central America. (Whitetails are also native to South America, and they have been introduced into New Zealand, the West Indies and Europe.)

The whitetails in North America include: northwestern whitetail, northeastern whitetail, southeastern whitetail, Texas whitetail, Coues whitetail, Mexican whitetail, and Central American whitetail. There is also the tiny Key whitetail, which is endangered and fully protected.

Before the various management programs were begun shortly after the turn of the century, the nation's whitetail population was at about 500,000. Today, they number close to 13 million, with an annual sport hunting harvest of over 2 million. And both the range and numbers of the animals continue to increase.

In the United States there are seasons for bowhunters that begin as early as August and extend through January. Bowyers are permitted in the field well in advance of the gun seasons, and these early-bird segments are usually of the either-sex sort. Archery equipment can also be used during the regular gun seasons, with the exception of some special hunts. Having an extra period gives bowhunters the chance to bag more animals. In some places this may be a single buck or doe, but there are a few states with extremely generous limits that allow many more to be legally harvested. One, for example, allows a deer a day, and another has no limit whatsoever.

That aspect certainly is appealing, but just as important to dedicated bowhunters is the luxury of being in the field without the noise and clamor that is generally associated with the gun season. All of the learned skills can be practiced without interruption, and the aesthetics of silence and solitude can be enjoyed to the fullest.

One final point about bowhunting the whitetail is that the interest in this species has broadened now to include many other big-game animals that were once almost exclusively sought with firearms.

## MULE DEER, BLACKTAIL DEER

While their ranges are much less extensive than the whitetail, mule deer and blacktail deer also offer bowhunters a great deal of opportunity, since collectively they occupy almost all of the western states. There are four species, with Rocky Mountain mule deer the most numerous. They are found in all or

*Mule deer*

parts of twenty-two states and southwestern Canada. The desert mule deer's range includes extreme southern California, parts of Arizona, New Mexico and Texas, and Baja California, northern Sonora, northern Chihuahua and northwestern Coahuila.

The Columbia blacktail deer occupies a narrow range along the Pacific Coast that extends from Bella Bella, British Columbia, in the north, including Vancouver Island and other offshore islands, to Monterey County, California, in the south. They have also been introduced on Kauai Island in Hawaii.

The Sitka blacktail deer occupies the most limited range of all, most of it along the coastal region of southwestern Alaska and British Columbia. They are also found on some offshore islands including the Queen Charlotte Islands, and have been introduced in some other islands in Prince William Sound, as well as Afognak and Kodiak Islands. In the case of these species, bowhunters usually get advantages in the way of earlier seasons and bag limits. In some places, the ranges of the whitetail deer, mule deer and blacktail deer overlap, and there are only a couple of small spots in the West where none of them are present.

# ELK

A bull elk is a trophy that practically every bowhunter in the country covets, and the numbers trying to get permits from the various western states that have hunts increases by leaps and bounds annually. Again, bowhunters get an early chance ahead of gun hunters, and it is usually during the peak bugling period when a good caller can bring an urgent bull to within easy bow range.

Elk were at one time found from the Atlantic to the Pacific Coasts, and from the Mexican border northward almost to the Arctic. Today, their range is spotty and vastly more limited, yet these trophy animals are the second most sought by American bowhunters.

There are four recognized species: Roosevelt elk, Tule elk, Rocky Mountain elk and Manitoba elk. Of these, the Rocky Mountain elk occupy by far the largest range, which includes the Rocky Mountain region of southeastern British Columbia and southwestern Alberta; eastern Washington and Oregon; Idaho; western Montana; Wyoming, southwestern South Dakota; northwestern Nebraska; northeastern Nevada; Utah, western Colorado; Arizona and

*Elk*

New Mexico. Limited introductions have been made in eleven eastern and western states, most of which offer no hunting opportunity.

Manitoba elk once occupied most of the prairie regions of Alberta to Manitoba, but they now are found at various locations in eastern Alberta and southern Saskatchewan and Manitoba, mainly in national and provincial park areas. Hunting opportunity for this species is very limited.

Tule elk are found only in California, where they once occupied large areas in the coastal and central parts of the state. Now, only several small herds exist within the original range. A transplanted herd in the Owens Valley provides the only Tule elk hunting opportunity, and this is by drawings for a limited number of permits issued annually.

The Roosevelt elk is the largest of them all, with bulls of up to 1,100 pounds having been taken. The range of this species is Vancouver Island in Canada, coastal Washington and Oregon, northwestern California, and an introduced population on Afognak and Raspberry Islands in Alaska. Some of the largest specimens are taken in the rain forests of Washington's Olympic Peninsula, which also offers some of the toughest hunting conditions.

Hunting tactics for elk are considerably different from those for whitetails, and there's also a greater challenge where shooting skills are concerned. Elk are big-bodied, and while they're as vulnerable as any other animals to arrows in the kill zone, a powerful bow, multi-bladed broadheads and pinpoint accuracy are important to success. Bowhunters score best during the bugling season, and since this begins fairly early in the fall, archery seasons often occur at the most ideal period.

The use of pack horses or four-wheel-drive vehicles in conjunction with elk hunts is highly desirable. Packing out a big bull is an extremely tough chore, yet the reward is great, since many people consider elk to be one of the most flavorful of all game meats.

# CARIBOU

In recent years, bowhunting for caribou has taken a giant leap forward in terms of popularity. Not only are these large-racked animals very abundant all across Canada, but in some places overpopulation has caused provincial governments to increase the bag limit to two caribou per hunter. Also, once aware of the great number of American archers who were seeking new adventures,

*Caribou*

numerous outfitters created bowhunting-only camps to allow them exclusive havens. It has been a boon for both parties.

Caribou are distributed throughout most of Alaska and Canada, and small fingers of range extend into northeastern Washington, northern Idaho and northwestern Montana.

There are six recognized caribou species, although some record keepers prefer to place them into three regional categories. Yet since there are some fairly major differences among them, it's worthwhile to have information on all six.

The Alaskan-Yukon Barren Ground caribou, found throughout most of Alaska, the Yukon and part of the Northwest Territories, is the most widely hunted of all the varieties. The migrating herds of animals sometimes number as many as 100,000. Visiting hunters take large numbers, but these animals are also a major source of food for natives, who depend on them for subsistence during the winter months.

The Central Canada Barren Ground caribou has a broad range that includes most of the Northwest Territories and parts of King William, Southhampton and Baffin Islands; and far northern Saskatchewan and Alberta. This species is a smaller race with simple antlers. The principal herds are the Baffin Island, Bathhurst, Beverly and Kaminuriak.

At one time, the Arctic Islands caribou was called Peary caribou, named after the Arctic explorer Admiral Robert F. Peary. This is the smallest of the caribou, and its range is the Arctic islands of the Northwest Territories, mainly Banks, Victoria, Prince of Wales and Somerset. Herds are small and tend to be mainly residential, and hunting them in these remote areas can offer some very severe conditions.

Mountain caribou are the largest species, weighing up to 600 pounds, and their heavy antler configuration makes them the favorite of many hunters. Their range includes the southern part of Yukon Territory; the southeastern part of the Northwest Territories; most of the eastern half of British Columbia, extending into Alberta; northern Alberta; and to a small extent into northeastern Washington, northern Idaho and northwestern Montana. Because of their preference for mountainous terrain, they're the most difficult to hunt.

Most of Quebec and Labrador have the species named for the region — Quebec-Labrador caribou — with the Ungava herd by far the largest. This race draws a lot of attention, since it is the one most accessible to hunters in the eastern U.S. Too, chances of success are very high, because their numbers have grown dramatically during the past ten years. Due to the increased competition for food, the herd is highly migratory, on the move most of the time throughout the year. This country is laced with lakes and waterways, and the principal hunting method is to locate crossings and intercept the animals. There are many outfitters in the Quebec-Labrador region that have camps restricted to archery only which attract huge numbers of bowhunters annually. The bag limit of two caribou per hunter is an added incentive. Quebec-Labrador caribou sometimes have spectacular racks.

Another species popular with eastern hunters is the woodland caribou. Found in small numbers in central Saskatchewan and Manitoba, a major herd is found in northern and central Ontario. There may also be small herds on the Gaspé Peninsula in Quebec and in New Brunswick and Nova Scotia. The best opportunity is on Newfoundland Island, but this is hunting on foot instead of by canoe, and it can be tough going.

# BEARS

"Once upon a time," as the bear story begins, these animals occupied almost all of Canada and the United States, and in the case of some kinds, their distribution is still fairly extensive.

Agriculture and deforestation have been the principal enemies of some bruins, while overhunting has definitely played the primary role in reducing the numbers of others kinds.

There are three major bear species: the American black bear, the brown-grizzly bear and the polar bear. Collectively, they are among the top three kinds of big-game animals sought by American hunters.

## AMERICAN BLACK BEAR

With the exception of the whitetail deer, the black bear has the most extensive range of the North American big-game animals. It also has the largest population of any bear species in the world. Because of this, it's logical that it is also the bear that gets the most attention from hunters, many of whom don't have to venture out of their home state.

*Black bear*

Black bears inhabit all of Alaska and Canada other than the extreme northern regions; the greater part of the western U.S. and into Mexico; the states around the Great Lakes; and the Ozarks, Appalachians, Florida and a narrow band of territory along the Gulf Coast that includes parts of Louisiana, Mississippi and Alabama.

This species has become a favorite of bowhunters, particularly in places where baiting is legal, since this provides an ideal situation for hunting from elevated stands. Outfitters have become acutely aware of this, and there are many camps that are strictly archery-only operations. Other methods—hunting with dogs or stillhunting—aren't as popular or productive.

## ALASKAN BROWN BEAR

No hunter who hasn't stood looking up at a standing mount of an Alaskan brown bear can fully appreciate how intimidating this animal can be, or what a challenge this species poses for bowhunters. Considered one of the top North American trophies, these big bruins are still sufficiently numerous to provide adequate opportunity. However, brown bear hunts are very expensive, and hunting conditions can be quite strenuous.

*Brown bear*

The range of this species is restricted to a narrow band of territory along the Alaskan coast and on adjacent islands where salmon runs occur. While this isn't its only food source, it is the most important one overall. Like all bears, it is omnivorous and feeds on whatever vegetable or animal matter is available, including carrion.

## GRIZZLY BEAR

The grizzly is the bear of legend, and its Latin name, *Ursus arctos horribilis*, seems especially appropriate. While perhaps no more dangerous or aggressive than either the Alaskan brown or the polar bear, its wider distribution and larger populations have always gained it more attention. Many tales of the Old West contained hair-raising accounts of humans in face-to-face encounters with ferocious grizzlies, and outdoor magazines once used these situations regularly for cover illustrations. Even today occasional encounters by campers or hikers are reported in the news.

In those pioneer days the range of this species was much larger, extending throughout all of western North America from Alaska to northern Mexico, and from the coast eastward to the Great Plains. Presently, the larger populations are in Canada and Alaska, with small pockets of grizzlies still remaining in Montana, Wyoming, Idaho and in Yellowstone National Park.

*Grizzly bear*

From a bowhunter's standpoint, next to the black bear, the grizzly offers the best prospects. This is because there is such a large range for hunting them. They can be sought in British Columbia, Saskatchewan, Yukon Territory, Northwest Territories and Alaska.

## POLAR BEAR

The most fearsome of all the bear species is the polar bear, which lives in an icy desert where food is scarce and anything that moves is regarded as a potential meal. A polar bear has no preference between a seal and a person, and unlike some other animals, it isn't deterred by the scent of man.

Some veteran hunters who have faced dangerous game animals in all parts of the world regard the white bear as the most ferocious and dangerous of them all. It is as large as the Alaskan brown, attaining weights of 800 to 1,000 pounds, but it vastly surpasses it in cunning and aggressiveness. These bears pose an enormous challenge to gun hunters but an even greater one to bowhunters. It took pioneer bowhunter Fred Bear three trips to the Arctic before he managed to take a polar bear with only his bow. He had put arrows into

*Polar bear*

bears on two earlier trips, but each had to be finished off with a rifle to avoid lethal consequences.

There is actually double jeopardy in this kind of sport: one from the treacherous bears and the other from the weather, which can be equally deadly.

## PRONGHORN ANTELOPE

These small, graceful animals offer bowhunters the chance to test many of their acquired skills, including stalking, the use of camouflage, and most of all, the ability to judge range and shoot accurately. Pronghorns are most often found in wide-open country with near-tabletop terrain, and they don't take cover. They're wary, though, so the matter of getting close enough is the problem.

The good news is that they're very plentiful, and in most places it's possible to conduct stalk after stalk until finally one pays off. Less widespread than in the past, their range is still very large, encompassing all or parts of Alberta, Saskatchewan, Oregon, Idaho, Nevada, California, Montana, Wyoming, Colorado, Arizona, New Mexico, North Dakota, Nebraska and Texas. The largest concentrations are in Wyoming.

*Pronghorn antelope*

Bowhunters should remember that the pronghorn is the fastest of the big-game animals. It can hit 60 mph in spurts and hold at well over 40 mph for long distances. Running shots are not recommended.

## NORTH AMERICAN SHEEP

There are two kinds of sheep on the North American continent: the American thinhorn sheep and the bighorn sheep, each of which has two species. In the thinhorn category are the Dall sheep and Stone sheep; in the bighorn category are the Rocky Mountain bighorn sheep and the desert bighorn sheep.

Many American hunters see wild sheep as the ultimate trophy, and collecting all four species for a "grand slam" is a feat every sheep fancier aspires to accomplish. It is extremely difficult for a gun hunter to do it and an even greater challenge for a bowhunter. It is also a very expensive trophy for both types of hunters.

*Bighorn sheep*

What makes this sport so tough is that in almost all instances sheep live in mountain country that's rugged, intimidating and physically demanding beyond what many hunters care to endure. Stalking at close ranges is very difficult and often dangerous.

## MOUNTAIN GOAT

Mountain goats live in the rugged mountains of the northern Rockies up through western Canada and Alaska. The difficult terrain they inhabit is usually their best defense against hunters. This type of hunting involves a serious physical commitment on the part of hunters—and often great expense.

Goat hunting is often very similar to sheep hunting: get up high and glass for animals. Once a trophy is spotted, hunters must stalk to within shooting range. Bowhunters who get above goats often have an advantage, as they rarely expect trouble from above. Shots can present themselves suddenly and at extreme angles; be sure you have practiced enough to be comfortable taking shots in these situations. A chance at a trophy billie is often a once-in-a-lifetime shot.

*Mountain goat*

# MOUNTAIN LION

Once hunted as varmints, mountain lions are now sought as trophy game animals in many western states. As their numbers have rebounded in recent years from historic lows, hunting opportunities have increased. These big cats are extremely wary and difficult to hunt; they have excellent eyesight and hearing and just seem to melt away into cover.

Putting dogs down on a fresh scent track is the best way to hunt lions. Once the dogs pick up the track, the chase is on. Some cats will tree very quickly, but they may jump and continue running, repeating the process many times until they either get away or stay put. It can be very difficult for bowhunters to get a clean shot at a treed cat that has worked its way up into thick branches. Arrow deflection can be a problem. A quick, clean-killing shot is very important, as a wounded mountain lion can pose a serious threat to hunters and dogs. Listening to the dogs work a lion can lead to a thrilling hunt or the ultimate wild goose chase, but when the opportunity does come for a shot at a treed cat, don't miss.

*Mountain lion*

# MOOSE

Moose range from New England across the northwest United States and throughout Canada and Alaska. The largest specimens are found in Alaska and western Canada, with the smaller Shiras moose inhabiting a range now extending south into parts of Colorado. The antlers on a bull moose can be very dramatic. The size of the palms, antler spread and number of tines increase each year until the bulls reach their prime at about six years of age. Although the moose has relatively poor eyesight it has a keen sense of smell and excellent hearing.

Stalking and stillhunting are effective techniques for bowhunters. During the rut, which coincides with most hunting seasons, aggressive bull moose can be called into shooting range. As the season progresses, valleys and wet bottomlands are good places to find animals. In the thick woods of eastern Canada and New England, finding a clear shooting lane can often be a tougher challenge than locating targets.

*Moose*

# WILD BOAR

These animals, also referred to as European wild boar or Russian wild boar, were first introduced into America in New York State in the 1880s. Later they were introduced into many more states, including North Carolina, Tennessee, West Virginia, Florida, California, Texas, New Hampshire and several coastal islands. However, interbreeding with domestic and feral hog stocks has destroyed all purebred stock except some held on a preserve on an island off Nova Scotia.

# FERAL BOAR

The feral boar preceded the appearance of the wild boar in America by many years. These hogs were brought into the country by Hernando de Soto as food sources for his exploration parties, and ones that escaped created the nucleus of the free-roaming feral hog population that's present today from coast to coast in no less than eighteen states.

These animals are particularly popular with hunters, since the abundance provides ample hunting opportunities. Many states consider these animals pests and have year-round open seasons on them with no limits. Other states class them as game and have special hunts where they can be hunted with dogs. There are also many commercial hunting preserves which operate on a year-round basis and are very popular with bowhunters, because they provide the chance for the thrill of hunting an animal that is tough, wily and dangerous in close quarters when wounded or cornered because of its sharp tusks. It also can add an impressive trophy to a collection.

# AFRICAN GAME ANIMALS

No place on earth is as intriguing and compelling to hunters as Africa, and with a constant progression of nations opening their doors to bowhunters, the potential continues to broaden. The acceptance of archery equipment has been accelerated as it becomes known that a bow in the hands of an accomplished hunter is a viable weapon for African game. The economic benefits no doubt also have persuasive powers.

The first significant bowhunting venture in modern times occurred in 1925 when Saxon Pope and Arthur Young made an expedition to what was then called Tanganyika. Until that time, the Dark Continent, as it was once called, had been ignored by bowyers from other countries since ancient times. Pope's classic book, *The Adventurous Bowmen*, tells of this:

> In the past other men have pursued African game with the bow and arrow. Every great Egyptian ruler seems to have on his tomb a record of his hunting exploits. There we see birds, jackals, gazelles and lions pieced by arrows. The Assyrian kings hunted lions in northern Syria; Assur Nasir-Pal shows us in bas-relief a picture of his hunting expeditions. He shoots from a racing chariot; beaters drive lions out of the jungle; arrow slain beasts lie on the ground about him; it is a royal hunt.
>
> Other rock engravings depict the king grasping a lion by the throat and stabbing him with a short sword. The beast is full of arrows and this is probably the death stroke. We have no reason to doubt the courage of the king, but there is a suggestion of dramatic license here.
>
> At least there is every evidence to prove that archers had invaded Africa long before our day. And, of course, we know there are millions of natives who use the bow and arrow in the wild of Ethiopia today as they have for thousands of years in the past.
>
> But since the epoch of the Crusades, no archers shooting the English long bow and the broadhead arrow have been in the country, and never to our knowledge has any representative of Robin Hood's Merrie Men ever loosed a flying shaft in that continent of mighty beasts. It was therefore with a profound feeling of the romantic significance of the event that we planned to carry the legend of the long bow into the jungles of Africa. We were to journey to the last stronghold of big game; we were to make a holy pilgrimage to the Mecca of all mighty hunters; we had set ourselves the task of vindicating the honor of the arms of our English forefathers with the yew bow and the broadhead arrow.

The Pope and Young expedition, although exciting and successful, had only minor impact outside a small group of archery buffs. Thirty years later, when interest in bowhunting had been revived and was rapidly gaining popularity, Africa was again visited. This time it was by Fred Bear, and on this first trip in 1955, and two subsequent ones in 1964 and 1965, he collected a broad array of game animals, including elephant, Cape buffalo, lion, kudu and many other kinds of antelope. His success in taking even the biggest and toughest animals was inspiration to bowyers.

Such exotic ventures may seem intimidating, but in truth, even bow-hunters with no big-game experience beyond whitetails needn't be discouraged from thinking about an African hunt. The broad gamut of game species available includes everything from the tiny blue duikers that weigh only about 8 pounds to the gigantic bull elephants that top 6 tons. With this kind of selection, it's simply a matter of choosing the size game one feels qualified to go after. You can learn big-game hunting as easily on African game as on what's available in the U.S., the difference being the cost in both time and money. Just the same, when it's considered that a reasonably priced safari can result in a hunter collecting a half-dozen or more small to medium-size animals in a single trip, the experience is not so difficult to justify.

## OTHER BIG-GAME OPPORTUNITIES

Africa is only one of the many places outside North America where there are excellent big-game opportunities available to bowhunters. South America has four native species and seven others that have been introduced. There are a dozen trophy animals in Europe that are indigenous, and three exotics. The continent of Asia has more than two dozen big-game animals, and with the greater access hunters now have to both Russia and China, an immense amount of previously off-limits territory has been opened up. A number of places in the South Pacific, Australia and New Zealand in particular, have good offerings of both medium-size and large animals.

# 6

# HUNTING BIG GAME

B ig-game hunting is something that places a great responsibility on the bowhunter, and it should not be undertaken until one possesses the confidence and skill necessary for effectively dealing with and killing the animals being sought.

A lot more than just the basics is required, and a serious bowhunter should undergo a rigorous training schedule before taking on big game. There is nothing more critical than the individual knowing *positively* what his or her maximum range is when it comes to placing shots. Some of the most heated and justified criticism of bowhunters—some of which is generated by bowhunters themselves—is the high incidence of hunters shooting at animals that are too far away. This can't be justified, and a truly conscientious bowhunter will avoid taking a long shot, no matter how tempting it may be.

The main thing is to recognize that everyone has limits, and these limits can increase with time and practice. However, the hunter's known capability at the time of the hunt is what must be considered. An easy way to determine the maximum range at which *dependable* accuracy can be achieved is to set up targets at various distances—20, 25, 30, 35 and 40 yards—and shoot five arrows at each. Then see which group is the tightest. Repeat this a few times and the answer will be evidenced in the results. Be sure your "test results" are current when you schedule a hunt.

Unlike some other sports where occasional handling of the equipment is sufficient to stay in top shape, bowhunters must practice constantly. There's no "off-season." A consistent regimen also pays off in improving accuracy, the ability to judge range and dexterity.

Shooting on ranges where authentic hunting conditions are duplicated permits hunters to broaden their skills and try new things. Some of the important skills: the ability to shoot well from all kinds of unusual positions, including prone; the ability to assess distances quickly and accurately; the ability to shoot through small openings in cover; and the ability to shoot accurately at moving targets.

## SHOOT TO KILL

Range judgment and shooting accuracy are important skills for hunting big game, but just as important is shot placement.

It's generally known and accepted that a hit in the heart/lung area will effect the quickest and cleanest kill. Of the two organs, the lungs are the best target to keep in mind. They occupy a much greater part of the rib cage than the heart, and when punctured by a broadhead there's always profuse bleeding. This is because the lungs are laced with a network of blood vessels, and when these are severed the lungs quickly fill and kill the animal or wound it severely.

Striking the heart will always kill the animal, but it presents a much smaller target. Also, in different species, the location differs slightly. The best plan is to aim for the area low on the chest and just behind the foreleg. That's easy on a broadside shot, but if the animal is standing in any other position, it's a different matter. Sometimes a heart/lung shot isn't possible, and an alternate must be decided upon.

The liver, lying to the rear of the lungs and forward of the stomach, can bring an animal down very quickly if the large arteries serving it are cut. If not, even though the wound will eventually be fatal, the animal may move for some distance before succumbing.

Those three—heart, lungs and liver—offer the spots that are the most vital in all big game. Some lucky hits, such as ones to the brain or spine, will usually bring about either an instant or relatively quick end. But they're not shots that should be attempted unless one is very certain of exact arrow placement.

Shots that sever any of the major arteries will result in death, although in some cases the animal may be able to put a lot of distance between itself and the hunter before collapsing. There are five of these large blood channels. The carotid travels up through the neck; the pyloric through the stomach; the renal-cavel to the liver; the aortic down the back; and the femoral down each of the back legs. However, they're slim vessels and can't be dependably targeted.

Hits at other places result in crippling the animal, and what occurs after this happens is determined by two things: the severity of the wound, and the hunter's reaction.

In almost every case, no matter where you think the arrow hit, simply sit tight and watch the animal to determine the line of flight. Listen carefully, too, because sometimes it will die and come crashing down within earshot.

After a little time has passed, it's okay to walk to where the animal was when you shot it and look for hair and blood. If your arrow passed through, there will definitely be evidence of both. If it didn't, the blood trail may not begin to show up at the site. Walk slowly along the path the animal took when fleeing, scrutinizing every inch of ground along the way. Sometimes blood sign may be no larger than a pinhead, and in some cases this may be all you have to go on for a considerable distance. Don't concentrate only on the ground, but look on shrubs and other vegetation where contact with the animal may have occurred.

There are telltale signs of where an arrow hit and what parts of the anatomy were damaged. Lung shots produce light red, frothy blood, as do shots to the carotid artery. Bright red blood indicates arterial bleeding, and dark red blood is from the liver or the renal artery. Finally, blood mixed with greenish or yellowish matter means a stomach shot, and while not always a lethal shot, the presence of blood increases the chances of recovering the animal.

In the case of deer, elk and similar animals, another clue is the kind of hair that's found. Shots low on the animal will shear light, short hair; medium brown hair will have come from the middle part of the body; and darker, coarser hair from higher on the animal.

The waiting period before following up wounded game should be at least twenty minutes, and the pursuit should be slow. If the blood trail is scanty or sporadic, it's a good idea to mark each new spot so that if you can't find another in the line you're traveling, you'll have a point of reference to which you can return and try again.

One exception to this wait-and-follow-slowly tactic is when you know the animal is hit in the leg or other spot where little bleeding will result. At such times a slow but steady pursuit should be initiated right away, traveling just fast enough to keep the animal on the move. If the blood doesn't coagulate, the animal may eventually weaken and go down.

## FIELD DRESSING GAME

No matter what kind of weather conditions or temperatures exist, it's important to field dress game soon after it is killed.

Unless you plan to hang the animal before field dressing it, you will need only a good, sharp hunting knife for the basic procedures. Only when it comes to quartering will a hatchet, axe or meat saw be needed. Other necessary accessories are some cloth and a plastic bag; and rubber surgeon's gloves for the cleaning process.

The first step is to make an incision around the anal vent, then pull it free and out until you can either tie it in a knot or tie it off with a string. This prevents fecal matter from getting into the body cavity when the intestinal tract is removed.

Next, with the animal on its back, open the entire cavity by making a cut from between the legs all the way to the base of the neck. Keep the cutting edge of the blade pointed upward, and use two fingers to guide the blade and hold the skin up to keep from puncturing the internal organs. Sever the windpipe where the cut ends.

At this point, try to locate the broadhead (if it hasn't exited) and remove it so as to avoid injury while field dressing, or problems later when the meat is cut up.

Once the cavity is open, roll the animal on its side and roll the contents out onto the ground. A cut will have to be made around the diaphragm that separates the stomach and intestines from the heart and liver. Pull them out and store them in the plastic bag. They're especially good to eat, and they will provide the first rewards to appear on the table.

The animal should then be rolled over and allowed to drain. When this has been completed, wipe the body cavity dry with a cloth.

Cooling the meat quickly is important. Hanging it is one of the best ways to do this, and if it can't be transported back to camp and hung right away, the body cavity should be propped open as wide as possible with sticks. In some cases it may be wise to skin and quarter the animal to expedite cooling. Many hunters carry cheesecloth in which to wrap meat and protect it from insects. The quarters can be hung up or laid out in cool, shady places.

Care of game meat from field dressing to the freezer makes a big difference in how it will fare on the table, so every step of the process should be conducted with this in mind. Delays in field dressing can be ruinous, and under some conditions bloating and spoilage may begin within an hour. Make sure all damaged tissue is trimmed off, and that all wound channels are free of bone splinters and hair.

## USING GAME MEAT

Game meat has always been considered a delicacy by many people who prefer it over domestically produced kind for reasons of taste alone. In addition, it's more nutritious and healthier, since it doesn't contain any chemical additives. This factor alone has been responsible for more people discovering the benefits and pleasures of game meat. And there are many families in North America that still rely on game as their primary food source. Looking back in America's history, there was a point when almost everyone did!

Paradoxically, today there are many people in the U.S. who don't hunt at all who benefit greatly from hunters' success. Because of the constantly growing whitetail deer herd and the need to manage it by allowing hunters more generous bag limits, there is a huge amount of venison harvested annually. Most hunters can't utilize as much as they can kill, so rather than waste animals, they stop hunting well short of their legal limits.

This doesn't have to happen anymore. Throughout the country various groups and organizations dedicated to feeding the homeless and hungry urge hunters to donate game meat to their organizations. The programs are very successful, and hunters have eagerly responded to the requests. It's an ideal plan, because it gives hunters both the incentive and a sound reason to harvest more game, plus the reward of knowing they have contributed to a very worthy cause. There's no trouble in finding out how to go about this. All that's required is a call to the state wildlife agency or its local representative.

## ACCESSORIES

Trying to identify all of the accessories available to the bowhunter would be an almost impossible task, because it seems the list of items grows almost daily. Many are essential, some are useful or needed only in certain situations, and others are of minimal value.

Certain things used with the hunting bow are small and incidental in appearance, yet being without them can spell the difference between success and failure. To name a few, there are string, cable, whisker and muff silencers that help prevent an animal from "jumping the string" at the moment the arrow is released. Also important are such accessories as camouflage suits, scents and calls.

**Mechanical releases** are preferred by many bowhunters because they eliminate the torque that invariably results from the finger release. There are a large number of variations and models, some using triggers and others levers or buttons to free the bowstring. Some veteran bowhunters shun releases because of the possibility of mechanical failure under certain conditions, but the majority of both target shooters and hunters now employ them.

An **arrow rest** assures that the released arrow begins its flight properly. In the old days (and possibly still used by some traditional longbow fans) a crooked finger or notch cut in the bow served this purpose. Today's bowhunter

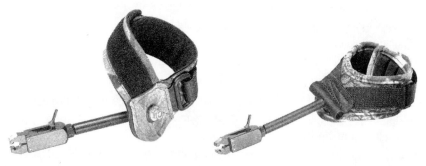

*Most bowhunters prefer to use a mechanical release.*

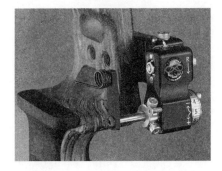

*A sampling of the many kinds of arrow rests available.*

can choose from a variety of devices that are much more suitable and convenient. There are two basic types: the launcher rests of the flipper/plunger design used by those who prefer the mechanical release; and the side-support rests favored by shooters using the finger release. Because there is a wide array of selections in both categories that can be confusing to a beginning bowhunter, it's best to choose a model recommended by an experienced archer or a pro shop.

**Stabilizers** are another way of dampening or eliminating torque and vibration by adding weight forward of the bow on the end of a metal rod. The weights vary from 6 to 16 ounces according to the shooter's needs. Target shooters use stabilizers that are up to 3 feet long, but stabilizers of less than 1 foot in length are preferred by bowhunters. Longer ones are cumbersome in field conditions.

 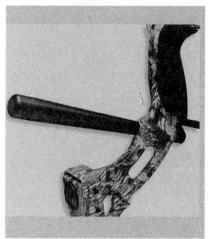

*Stabilizers come in a variety of shapes, sizes, and materials.*

Hunters operating from tree stands always leave their shooting equipment on the ground to avoid accidents while ascending. A **bow hoist** is handy for this purpose, because it can be attached to either the hunter's belt or the stand. The stout nylon twine is attached to the equipment, and as it is raised, the spring-loaded reel stores the line to prevent tangling and snagging.

Bowhunters who also hunt with rifles are often more comfortable and confident using **peep sights** because of the similarity to the gunsight system. The peep, mounted in the bowstring, is much like the rear sight of a rifle and gives the shooter assurance of identical alignment with the eye to the bowsight each time.

**Binoculars** can be one of a bowhunter's best friends in the field, not only for scanning for game, but also for scrutinizing shooting lanes for any obstacles not visible to the unaided eye. There are numerous small, compact models that can be tucked into a shirt or jacket pocket. The best of these have good light-gathering qualities for dawn or dusk viewing. Binoculars serve another purpose, too, which is to provide enjoyment and pleasure by being able to observe wildlife activities that otherwise might be overlooked.

**Rangefinders** can be very valuable, also, since this form of optics permits the accurate measurement of distance from the bowhunter to the target

*Some archers like bowstring peep sights. This one incorporates light-catching fiber optics for low-light shooting.*

or to other objects near a stand that can serve as yardage markers. One of these devices developed especially for bowhunters is only 2¼" × 2¼" × ½" in size, and 2 ounces in weight. Another is only slightly larger and weighs 5 ounces.

Whether you're hunting from a stand or the ground, a light **folding saw** will make clearing shooting lanes or trimming branches for climbing stands a

*Bowhunter-friendly backpacks have come a long way. This waterproof pack protects arrow rests and sights and has a quick-release system for easy access.*

Compact rangefinders are a big help in determining distance to the target with great accuracy.

lot easier. They don't take up much room in a jacket or day pack, and they're well worth the space.

A **flashlight** is an essential for hunters, since most often they're going out or coming back in the dark. There are also a variety of headlamps available that offer a strong light source and allow hunters to keep both hands free.

Choosing the right **knife** depends mainly on how you will use it. Sometimes the best idea is to have more than one as standard equipment. A fairly small folder is adequate for field dressing most small game, and it sometimes is sufficient to handle medium-size animals such as whitetail deer or antelope. However, if either the pelvic or breast areas need to be opened, an alternate saw-tooth blade is necessary to do the job well.

A good pair of binoculars is essential for bowhunters.

## BOWHUNTING *BIG* BIG GAME
By M. R. James
*Kalispell, Montana*

Sooner or later most experienced deer hunters start dreaming of a hunt for big-antlered bull elk, moose or caribou. And what veteran black bear hunter hasn't imagined drawing an arrow on a big-bodied grizzly or brown bear? Modern-day bowhunters venture as far as Alaska and Africa to tag the biggest and baddest of the world's big-game animals. Here are some time-tested tips:

Shoot the heaviest pulling bow you can shoot accurately, but don't over-bow yourself. A well-placed arrow from a 65- or 70-pound bow is better than a bad hit—or complete miss—with a bow pulling 90 or more pounds. Proper arrow placement is the key.

Always aim for the animal's heart/lung area. A double-lung hit is a bowhunter's most deadly shot. Wait to release until the animal is broadside or quartering slightly away. Never rush your shot.

"Pick a spot" is advice worth repeating to all bowhunters drawing down on bigger animals. It seems that the bigger the target the easier it is to forget this common-sense rule. Aiming at the entire animal is the surest way to miss. Think small to score big.

Never use a broadhead that isn't shaving-sharp. Look to sturdy, well-constructed heads that fly true from your hunting bow. Well ahead of the actual hunt, practice shooting with broadheads only.

Learn your effective shooting range and take all shots within the self-imposed yardage limitations. Always resist the temptation to take an iffy shot. Patience pays.

Finally, realize that most big-game animals—whether a 200-pound mule deer buck or a 1,400-pound bull moose—are taken by bowhunters at ranges of 30 yards or less. Always work to get as close as possible to your quarry, unseen and unheard, then make that first shot count.

*M. R. James is editor/publisher of* Bowhunter Magazine *and is an award-winning writer and public speaker (with the PBS and OWAA Speakers' Bureau) who's been bowhunting for more than thirty years. He took his first Pope & Young animal in 1963 and has several in the P&Y record book. He has written several books and hundreds of magazine articles. He is currently first vice president, senior member and official measurer of the Pope & Young Club; and he is director of the National Bowhunter Education Foundation, and of Bowhunters of America.*

*There are enough knives available to satisfy even the most particular hunter.*

For big animals like elk or caribou or bears, nothing beats a big, broad-bladed, one-piece knife and a good whetstone for the occasional sharpening required when working with thick, tough skin. And the companion tool should be one of the compact **heavy-duty saws** that hunters use for many different camp tasks. An alternative is a holstered **knife/hatchet combination.**

A cold or wet "behind" hampers a hunter's powers of concentration, not to mention being downright uncomfortable. That's why it's a good idea to carry along a light **cushion.** There is a wide variety, some that are solid, others filled with shredded materials, and one that is a cloth-covered innertube that can be inflated to whatever degree of firmness the hunter prefers.

It's smart and sometimes necessary to mark trails that have to be followed into stands or other pre-selected spots in darkness. Some hunters carry a roll of **red** or **blaze orange survey tape** for this purpose, and although it's effective, it also points the way for other hunters to your "honey hole." Another method is the use of the little **thumbtacks** that can be pushed into a tree. They glow brightly in a flashlight beam, but unlike the tape, they're very unobtrusive in the daytime.

Sophisticated **sound amplifiers** have been developed in recent years that can help a hunter hear sounds in the woods long before they would otherwise be audible. This can help identify the direction from which an animal or bird is approaching or determine if it's something other than what's being sought. This is an outgrowth, or new application, of the devices that have long been used to listen to and record birdsongs.

Position in this list of accessories doesn't have anything to do with order of importance. If it did, the suggestion that the use of a **game tracker** for white-

*Sound amplification devices give hunters an edge in the woods. This one can be custom set to match specific sound frequences.*

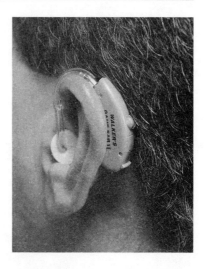

tail deer, black bear and wild turkey would have appeared earlier. The device is a cylinder that mounts on the bow and which holds up to 2,500 feet of 17-pound-test nylon line. The end of the line is attached to the arrow, and if the animal or bird runs or flies when hit, the line pays out. You then simply follow the line to find your quarry. It's of particular value near dark when you can't see your arrow or when rain washes out a blood trail. Some outfitters insist that all clients use this device as a way to reduce losses, and some even refer to it as a "game saver."

Night tracking can be greatly assisted with a **high-powered light** that generates up to 500,000 units of candlepower. An alternate to bright illumina-

*Fire tacks were developed to help hunters mark their trail. They glow when hit with the beam of a flashlight.*

*A first aid kit can be a true lifesaver.*

tion (which can cause too much disturbance in the field) is a less-bright light with a red lens that doesn't frighten game. And a substance is now available that turns blood on a game trail fluorescent, so it has utility in both daytime and nocturnal situations.

The threat of Lyme disease has made hunters acutely aware of the dangers ticks pose, so at times of the year when these pests are present, it's important to carry along the right **repellent**. There's also a compact kit on the market that has the items needed for safe tick removal. As far as other insect repellents are concerned, some big-game hunters shun them because of their odor. Of course, the odor factor has no bearing whatsoever on many kinds of

*GPS devices are now affordable and easy to carry in the field. Backcountry hunters, particularly those venturing into new territory, would be wise to pack one along.*

game sought by bowhunters. Wild turkeys are a good example, and the thought of hunting them in the spring in many parts of the South without repellent makes one cringe! The same goes for spring bear hunting in blackfly country, or seeking caribou on the tundra in early season when both blackflies and mosquitoes are still swarming everywhere.

There's an element of danger present whenever a hunter is afield, and every bowhunter should carry a basic **tool kit** with the items necessary for replacement or repair, but in addition, having a basic **emergency kit** can be extremely important.

## CAMOUFLAGE

It would be impossible for most hunters to imagine going afield without camouflage, because it has become such a vital element in so many types of big-game, small-game and waterfowl hunting throughout the country. It's even used in some situations where it offers no advantage other than making the individual feel more a part of the environment.

*Camouflage is an important asset to a bowhunter, especially when the right pattern is selected.*

Prior to World War II, commercially produced camouflage was unknown to hunters. They wore clothes of the color that best matched or blended with whatever situation they were in, and they used natural materials to further enhance their efforts to be unseen. The big change came when war surplus outlets offered clothing, netting and other items in military camouflage patterns. This was a veritable boon for hunters, and it created an appetite that has become insatiable. Today, there's hardly any hunting item that isn't available in camouflage, including camouflaged toilet paper and a host of other products that border on being little more than gimmicks.

There's also some question of judgment when considering how far the camouflage concept should be carried. Little things like mini-flashlights, diaphragm turkey call holders, pens and pencils are very hard to spot if lost or dropped in the woods, and in these cases it seems logical that blaze orange or some other highly visible color should be used.

Several factors have contributed to the enormous growth of the camouflage industry, one of which has been the huge expansion of whitetail and turkey populations that has provided hunters with vastly more opportunity.

*Camouflage blinds help hunters blend into their surroundings.*

Since camouflage is regarded as vital for pursuing both species, the demand has increased correspondingly.

There has also been a continuing insistence for innovations and improvements in both equipment and clothing, and it is in this area that bowhunters have played a significant role. Bowhunters have a greater dependency on excellence in things that contribute to their ability to be stealthy and well concealed, since they must approach game closely in order to be successful. They're particularly discriminating in selecting equipment and accessories, and their constantly growing impact on the economy of the outdoor industry has given manufacturers additional impetus to develop materials and designs suited for their needs.

The advancements have been notable. Once manufacturers departed from the military camouflage concept, new ideas emerged. One of the first was a design simulating tree bark that was very suitable for hunting in deciduous forests. That opened a floodgate of both imitators and innovators, and what emerged has been a succession of new patterns too numerous to list. You name it, and there's almost certainly a type to fit the situation, not only in appearance, but also in suitable weight for whatever climate condition exists. Snow? No trouble. Dry, arid desert? Sure. Marsh grass, bottomland hardwood timber, pine forests or whatever? No problem. Additionally, many kinds are offered in color variations that key in with seasonal foliage changes.

There's been another very notable advance, and one for which bowhunters can take a great deal of credit: the development of hunting clothes made of soft fabrics that make moving in the woods vastly more quiet than when wearing garments of the traditional textiles. To bowhunters, silence is indeed golden, and no other breed of hunters has to depend upon it so heavily.

Dozens of choices in camouflaged boots and hats are on the market, so this becomes a matter of individual preferences and the situations or conditions in which they will be used. Other things that assist in the bowhunter's quest for invisibility are those which hide the face, the hands and all equipment items that are visible. There are even treatments for clothing that make it impossible for deer to see the ultraviolet light that is supposed to cause a hunter's clothing to glow.

Hiding the face and hands is essential, and there are two main ways to go about this. Head nets and face masks are popular. Some fit loosely over the face

*Three-dimensional camouflage can effectively alter a hunter's body form.*

and others made of tightly woven material fit skintight. The alternative is camouflage greasepaint that allows a hunter to create patterns for each situation and alter them in the field as the situation may warrant. As for the hands, gloves can be used, but many bowhunters prefer greasepaint, since it doesn't impair the delicate feel for the bowstring they need when shooting. However, tight-fitting, finger-like gloves work well and are especially desirable in cold weather.

Most hunting bows, arrows and quivers are now offered in camouflage, and those that aren't can be easily disguised with either spray paint or tape.

And just to prove that there's almost no limit to how far the camouflage concept can be carried, "breath camouflage" can be obtained in both liquid and chewing-gum form.

## SCENT

Long before it became a major part of either the gun hunting or bowhunting scene, scent was understood and utilized by trappers, and it was from this base of accumulated information that the industry and individuals got a head start on putting it to other uses.

---

### USING SCENTS AND OTHER TIPS
By Wayne Pearson
*Naylor, Georgia*

Over the past few years, I've harvested several Boone & Crockett and Pope & Young record-book animals. There are many ingredients for success. You have to hunt an area which holds big bucks. Pre-scouting is a must, and you must get to know your area well.

Keep wind intensity and direction in mind, and place your stand according to the prevailing winds. Allow ample time for the deer to become accustomed to your stand. Generally, the higher you are, the better. I like to get at least sixteen feet up the tree. Be sure to always use a safety belt.

Approach your stand early in the day, allowing time for the woods to settle. Pack a lunch so you can hunt all day. You may only have one opportunity for that really big buck, so I suggest wearing rubber boots to help eliminate odors. I use a scent product called B-Scent Free Spray from Johnson Labs. It actually eliminates human odor by neutralizing odor-causing bacteria.

Also, I wash my hunting clothes in baking soda, and I use unscented soaps and deodorants. Keep your hair smoke-free and your body clean.

I have harvested a lot of nice bucks by rattling and using grunt tubes, but for a record-book-class buck I leave my horns and tubes at home. A trophy buck didn't get that big by being stupid, and you can't afford to alert him in any way.

So, remember: clean clothes, clean body, proper stand placement, wind direction, good scouting, good coverup (B-Scent or comparable), rubber boots, and plenty of dedication. Use these tips, hunt long and hard, and you will be successful.

Good luck with your hunting.

*Wayne Pearson is widely known as the host of* Ultimate Outdoor Experiences with Wayne Pearson *on ESPN. Responding to viewer requests for an outdoor club, the Lancaster/Outdoor Trail Sportsman Club was formed. Members receive a quarterly publication and are eligible to win free hunting and fishing trips. Wayne is a lifelong outdoorsman who has several Boone & Crockett and Pope & Young animals—deer and antelope—to his credit. He is proudest of his Double Grand Slam on wild turkeys (two each of four separate species in one season).*

---

*A hunter applies mock scrape gel to attract whitetails.*

Basically, there are two kinds of scents: those that attract or lure, and those that mask or cover odors. Deer and some other big-game animals find human odor frightening, and encountering a human scent causes them to avoid the source. It's also understood that some odors are attractive to these animals, especially those that relate to creatures of the opposite sex at certain times of the year.

Bowhunters have more at stake where scents are concerned because they must get close to game, so they go the extra mile to be sure that what they select works.

Those scents that attract animals can be ones related to food types, which are useful at any time during the season. During the rut period, sex or musk scents work the best. This entails the use of one or more of the substances and materials for this purpose. There are many, but the most common are: doe in heat, tarsal gland, fresh trail, mock scrape, deer pellets, estrus and things that combine more than one of these elements.

Even when using these kinds of scents, it's still advisable to use cover scents, too, because if human odor is present, it can override the other types of scents and affect the animal.

*A wide variety of attractant scents and scent-blocking products are available.*

Cover scents can be odors that smell natural to the animal, or even a neutral odor that isn't identifiable. The effectiveness of any kind of scent can be much improved by bathing the night before with a non-perfumed, anti-bacterial soap and wearing clean clothing washed in one of the soaps available in sporting goods stores that leave no detectable odor. Effective, also, are scent-eliminator sprays that can be applied in the field as an additional assurance of non-smell.

Cover scents can be applied to clothing, boots or the skin, and this is usually done before entering the woods in order to prevent leaving an odor trail. Much of the camouflage clothing available today incorporates scent-blocking technology, as well. Attractants should never be used in this manner. They should be applied at the site, but distant from the stand so the deer's delicate nose can't pinpoint the hunter's exact location. Wind direction and other factors will determine where the scent should be located. For additional insurance, cover scents can be also placed in the vicinity of the stand.

Remember that when stalking or stillhunting you must be aware of your odor. A scent that masks it is effective when you're on the move. The ones to use are what works best for you, and there are some very successful hunters who concoct their own formulas with natural materials and don't rely on any of the commercial products.

## USING GRUNT CALLS
Peter J. Fiduccia
*Warwick, New York*

*Peter Fiduccia using a grunt call. Blow the call gently, and don't use it too frequently.*

The secret to being a successful caller of whitetail deer is confidence. Knowing that your call sounds authentic and believing it can lure in deer are critical to your success. Confidence can mean the difference between seeing and actually bagging game on a consistent basis.

Hunters can effectively replicate several different types of deer vocalizations. One of the most common, and easiest to learn, is the grunt of does and bucks. Grunting occurs throughout the year. Hunters will have optimum success, however, when they imitate the grunt of a buck in rut. The best response to grunting will come between late October and mid-November, and again in mid-December. Grunting reaches its peak when both bucks and does are chasing each other or freshening scrapes during the peak rut. For the grunt call to work most effectively, it should be blown gently. If it is not, you will scare off more bucks than you will attract. Even trophy-sized bucks will sometimes avoid a conflict if they're hot on the trail of a doe. Smaller bucks are definitely intimidated by deeper guttural grunts, which bigger bucks generally make.

Most whitetail hunters compare the grunts they have heard to sounds made by a domestic pig. Others describe grunts as sounding like burps. Both are correct. A doe grunt is longer in duration and sounds like, "Aaaaaahhhhhhhhhh." The grunt of a buck on the trail of a doe in estrus sounds like a short burp, "Erp-Erp . . . Erp-Erp . . . Erp-Erp." When a hunter hears and sees a buck making this grunt, his best response is to blow two short burp-grunts back. Usually, the buck will lift his head and go straight for what he believes to be another buck on the trail of "his" doe. When you do not see or hear a buck, and want to attract one, extend the length of the call, "Eeeeerrrrpp . . . Eeeeerrrrpp." You will know immediately if you are blowing the call incorrectly if your call sounds like a duck call. Hunters who use the grunt will find it easy to use and one of their most successful calls for attracting bucks to their stands.

*Peter Fiduccia is Editor in Chief of the Outdoorsman's Edge Book Club; host of the TV series,* Woods 'n Waters; *author of the books* Whitetail Strategies *and* 101 Deer Hunting Tips; *and co-author, with Jay Cassell, of* The Quotable Hunter *and* North America's Greatest Whitetail Lodges and Outfitters.

## CALLS

Attracting big-game animals with sounds of various sorts isn't anything new to hunters. Elk and moose calls are traditional, and in some parts of the country, rattling for mule and whitetail deer has in the last few years gained great popularity and a large following as an effective tactic for luring in big bucks during the mating season.

However, the increased attention now being paid to deer vocalization, primarily in whitetails, has caused hunters to regard a deer call as essential and one of their top priorities. It's been adequately proven that the use of these devices can provide a big advantage in that they lure deer into closer range, and this has given bowhunters special reason to want to learn to use them.

In all calls, the signals sent consist of everything from greetings to challenges, and from invitations to play around to cries of distress or injury. Sometimes, they are successful by doing nothing more than arousing the animal's curiosity and causing it to investigate what's going on.

*Horn rattling is a very productive method of calling in bucks during the rut. Having a friend handle the rattling will allow you to concentrate on shooting with a minimum of movement.*

*Buck boards (left) provide a handy substitute to rattling with a bulky pair of antlers. The grunt call (right) has become very popular as a way of imitating various kinds of deer vocalizations.*

There are numerous mechanisms for producing the various sounds deer use to communicate, but the ones that have been found to be the most effective calls are the reed-type "grunt calls" that provide the most authentic reproductions of "deer talk."

# 7

# TREE STANDS

The idea of hunting game from an elevated position isn't anything new, because early man found tree limbs ideal spots from which to drop big rocks or hurl spears at animals passing underneath. Since some of the creatures they sought were dangerous, the method proved to be safe as well.

Using this tactic of staying out of harm's way while hunting became more sophisticated over the centuries. Instead of simply perching on a limb, hunters built structures in which to sit that provided both better concealment and a larger degree of comfort. In Africa and India they were used mainly when seeking lions and tigers, but they also began to appear in parts of Europe where red stag and various kinds of deer were hunted.

The European models were usually tower-like wooden platforms that either stood independently or were built in or against trees. More often than not, they were built to accommodate from two to four people. The advantage wasn't safety, but increased visibility.

Some of the early stands used in America followed this pattern, but just as common were very simple structures that sometimes consisted of little more than a couple of planks nailed across parallel limbs and a series of spikes or wooden crosspieces to climb to the perch.

With the appearance of portable stands, the use of wooden structures began to diminish. For one thing, they were permanently attached and in time could deteriorate and become unsafe. Also they weren't aesthetically pleasing. But more important, they did damage to trees. Because of this, they were declared illegal on federal lands, as well as on many state and timber company holdings.

Portable stands are extremely popular among big-game hunters in different parts of the country, but especially so in the eastern United States where whitetail deer are the principal species sought. They're particularly favored by bowhunters, and to say that perhaps 80 percent use them would be a conservative estimate. This is because being situated well above ground level allows a bowhunter to be more effective in a number of ways. It allows the hunter to be

*Scouting before the season to find the right spot for a tree stand is very important. Portable stands make setting up a breeze.*

*Small stands like this one with detachable ladder steps can be carried anywhere in a backpack.*

less obtrusive and improves the chances of game coming into closer proximity. Too, certain locations will offer better shooting lanes than can be obtained by removing a few limbs or branches, so deciding where and how to place a stand should be given careful consideration.

Deer don't always look up, so the odds favor bowhunters seeking this species, but when it comes to wild turkeys, which look everywhere, you're sometimes just as well off in a ground blind.

There are enough kinds of stands on the market today to offer the bowhunter every kind of option imaginable, and in virtually every price range. Some of the basic types are little more than metal frames that strap to a tree and cost only a few dollars. On the other end of the line are big, comfortable stands with padded seats and other special features that are quite expensive. However, with the intense focus of attention on safety, almost all manufacturers use high-tech materials and the best designs to address this concern. It should be remembered, though, that anytime one is situated high above the ground there is a danger factor, and avoiding accidents is the individual hunter's responsibility.

# STAND HUNTING TACTICS
By Jay Cassell
*Katonah, New York*

*Jay Cassell with 10-pointer he took from a treestand in New York's Catskill Mountains*

When I hike through the woods, scouting prior to the season, I look for candidates for my treestands. In particular, I search for trees that overlook frequently used deer trails, paths that either lead from bedding areas and heavy cover to obvious food sources, or paths that go through gullies, ravines, and other natural funnels in the terrain. I also look for a tree that's at least 10 yards off my chosen trail; if you set up a treestand too close to a trail, deer will peg you in a hurry. Search for a relatively straight tree, one whose diameter is right for the size of your stand (of special importance if you're using a climber). Additionally, find a tree near others trees that will break up your silhouette. The last thing you want to do is set your stand in a tree that's all by itself, no matter how ideally located it may be to a trail. Deer will spot you from a mile away in such a solitary tree.

If you find a tree you like, set up your stand (or make a mental note of that tree, and come back with your climber once the season starts). Make sure your lock-on is secure, and that the steps are evenly spaced so you don't have to be a contortionist to get up onto your platform. If you are hunting in an area where other people might come by, consider using a kryptonite lock to discourage theft.

Next, devise a routine and stick with it each time you go afield. If you know where your gear always is—big or small—you have fewer chances for making mistakes or losing things. My routine is this: Before I start into the woods, I strap my safety belt around my waist. The part of the belt that goes around the tree is in my left pocket; my release is in my right pocket. Every other piece of gear I need for the day is in my backpack.

When I get to my tree—and I take awhile to get there, in case some deer might be nearby—I first tie my bow to the tow rope. Then I strap my safety belt around the tree, and up I go, step by step, until I reach the platform. Once I get into my stand, I secure my safety belt, hang my backpack on the hook that I always insert off to the side of my stand, then I haul up my bow, and settle in.

While in the tree, I keep my movements to a minimum. If it's cold, I make sure that I have enough clothes on so that I don't start to fidget around, trying to keep warm. Chemical hand warmers always come in handy, especially since I really don't like to wear a glove on my release hand. And then I stick it out —either until lunch time, or dark, when I reverse my routine, and make my way down the tree, and out of the woods.

*Jay Cassell is Senior Editor of the Lyons Press, and has written a number of books on hunting, including* The Quotable Hunter *and* North America's Greatest Whitetail Lodges and Outfitters *(both co-authored with Peter Fiduccia), as well as* North America's Greatest Big Game Lodges and Outfitters *(co-authored with John Ross.)*

# CLIMBING STANDS

One of the first commercial models to be introduced was the two-piece climbing stand, which operates on a sort of inchworm principle. Both sections are attached around the trunk, with a sharp or serrated blade that will bite into the bark when pressure is placed on it. The hunter stands on the lower part, raises the upper part with the arms and puts it solidly in position, then repeats the process with the lower unit. A safety belt is a must for this or any other kind of climbing operation.

Until quite recently, these stands required trees with straight trunks and no limbs to interfere with the climb. If some were present between the ground and the height the hunter wished to attain, they had to first be removed. However, climbers with separate units for each foot that permit a hunter to simply climb around and past limbs are now available.

Because the original climbing stands, as well as some still currently available, can do damage to trees, they are illegal to use in many forest areas.

*A full-body harness and safety belt are a good idea in any tree stand. A quick-release mechanism makes clicking in a snap.*

This ban has caused significant changes in design, and many of these modified climbers no longer present a hazard to the resource and are environmentally acceptable.

## STRAP-ON STANDS

Strap-on and chain-on stands have advantages over the climbers because they can be placed almost anywhere on the trunk, and there is one model that can be set up like a stool on horizontal limbs. They also don't draw fire from the game agencies and timber companies, since the methods of attachment aren't detrimental to the trees. What has caused problems are the procedures used to climb the trees to put the stands in place. One popular way is with metal screw-in steps, which are sturdy and safe. Still, they also do tree damage, and this has led to their being outlawed in many places. Again, industry responded quickly and satisfactorily with strap-on steps that use only nylon webbing to hold them in place. They're easier and quicker to

*Strap-on ladder steps like these are easy to set up and don't damage trees like earlier models.*

*Screw-in steps like the one on the left are convenient, but quick-release strap-on steps are also quick to place and don't damage trees.*

attach than the metal ones, and if a hunter wants to add a measure of protection, they can be quickly removed upon departure, leaving no access to the stand.

Another practical device to use in conjunction with these kinds of stands is a lightweight, sectional metal tube with steps that can be strapped to a tree to erect the stand, and to use getting in and out. As with the strap-on steps, it can be taken down each day after the hunt and either carried out or hidden nearby.

*Glow caps can help hunters find their footing while ascending and descending stands in darkness. They glow when illuminated with a flashlight.*

*Modern tree stands come with many accessories like this bow holder.*

# LADDER STANDS

Ladder stands are one of the most convenient of all, because they are simple to erect, don't require any steps to be put in place, and can be quickly and easily moved from one location to another. They're also safe and comfortable, and most manufactured models have sectional legs that allow them to be erected at whatever level is desired. Some commercial deer hunting operations use ladder stands made of wood that serve the same purpose, but which aren't as portable.

These kinds of stands run the gamut from the simple to the fancy, and some on the high end of the spectrum have camouflaged skirts around the platform to hide the hunter and even umbrellas to protect him from the rain.

# TRIPOD STANDS

The three-legged tripod stand can be very important in providing bowhunters with an elevated position at clear-cuts or other locations where there are no trees present. They're not as easily moved around as other stands, but if placed in an area where there will be deer activity throughout the season, this isn't necessary, anyway.

*This hunter is clearing a shooting lane around his stand.*

The swivel seats on these stands give a hunter 360-degree visual and shooting potential, and it's possible to shoot from either a sitting or standing position. Most tripod stands have either a standard or optional metal bar surrounding the hunter to which camouflaged skirts can be added.

Telescoping legs make it possible to adjust these stands on uneven ground, but it's wise to consider them as somewhat unstable under any conditions. An abrupt movement by the hunter or gust of wind is sometimes enough to tip them over. To safeguard against this, drive a wood or metal stake at the base of each leg and secure the two together with rope. That eliminates the threat of falling and guarantees peace of mind.

Because elevated stands cause the major part of injuries hunters suffer in the field, many hunting camp operators take extra precautions regarding their use. They have the welfare of their clients at heart, and aside from personal feelings, there's the matter of liability claims that could be leveled against them.

One way some operators reduce the chance of such accidents is by having their guides assist getting hunters in place and making sure their safety belts are properly attached. The hunters are supposed to remain in the stand

*Many tree stands can be adjusted to accommodate standing or sitting hunters.*

until the guide returns. That covers two-thirds of the potentially dangerous period, and the rest is up to the individual hunter.

The matter of liability is a subject that causes manufacturers of stands to cringe, since many lawsuits of this sort have been brought against them. As a result, some companies have been driven out of business and others have been financially crippled. In some instances manufacturers have been at fault, while in others hunter error has been the bigger factor.

One good result has been a concerned effort on the part of manufacturers to make stands as safe and sound as possible. Plenty of progress has been made through the use of high-tech materials and innovative engineering. Still, the responsibility for stand selection and its proper use remains with the hunter.

# STALKING

O ther than being able to shoot well, there is no skill more important to becoming a fully qualified, all-around bowhunter than being able to stalk, or as some refer to it, stillhunt.

This is the ability to seek out game instead of waiting for it to come to you, and to match wits with the animal on a one-on-one basis. It's an especially rewarding kind of hunting that creates an immense sense of self-satisfaction. There's a special thrill and feeling of accomplishment when you are standing over a nice buck you've bagged by being able to get within shooting range, or an antelope that has required a long, slow, inch-by-inch approach over open country.

For the bowhunter who plans to seek several kinds of game, a talent for stalking is an absolute necessity. There are many animals, large and small, that you have to go after. They can't be collected by sitting in a stand or a blind.

# MOVING QUIETLY

Silence is truly of great importance when it comes to moving on the ground, and if there is any term that best describes how to do it, it is "cat-like."

Think of it for a moment and you'll see why. You've no doubt seen a cat stalking a mouse or a bird, and noticed the way it behaves in the process.

First of all, it approaches its prey very slowly, instantly freezing in place if the prey looks in its direction. Second, it places its paws down softly and carefully in order to avoid making any sound. And all the while it is concentrating completely on the creature it is stalking.

Remember how, as a kid, you liked to sneak up on playmates and surprise them. The main difference in hunting is that animals are more alert and harder to slip up on than humans. Also, conditions in the woods like dry leaves, twigs or thick understory growth make moving silently a great deal more difficult. More often than not, it's a one-step-at-a-time process, studying every spot before putting a foot down on it. Progress can be agonizingly slow at times, but there's no alternate way to success.

Looking at it from another perspective, sounds aren't always a nemesis, because there are some that don't alarm animals and which you can use as an advantage. Things like planes passing over, the buzz of a chain saw, a train whistle, barking dogs, crows calling or other noises provide a mask for any sounds you may make as you move. Some creatures create their own baffles against outside sounds. When squirrels are cutting nuts, they can't hear much except their own endeavors. The same applies to gobbling turkeys or bugling elk. By acting quickly when such opportunities present themselves, you can gain a few extra yards, which at times can be very precious!

A basic formula for stalking is to take three or four slow, careful steps, then stop for at least a full minute, scanning everything around and listening intently. If you're serious about learning this technique, you must remember there are no shortcuts, and time shouldn't be of consequence.

Concentration is required throughout, of course, but like the cat, you must always have your "eye on the sparrow," whether or not it's in sight. If you can see the quarry, then you will be zeroed in on it every second, constantly shaping your strategy according to what it is doing, and trying to anticipate what it might do next. If you haven't seen it yet, then it's imperative that everything in front of you be minutely examined before each forward step.

*This bowhunter used stealth and camouflage to line up a shot at a nice whitetail buck.*

Finally, becoming an accomplished stillhunter doesn't happen overnight, and the only way to attain any degree of proficiency is to practice. One of the best ways for beginners to learn is to go squirrel hunting. Stalking bushytails involves all of the elements needed for hunting virtually any kind of game, large or small. You don't even have to shoot: just see if you can get to where you could if you wanted to.

## USING THE WIND

Perhaps the most quixotic element a hunter stalking big game has to contend with is the wind. Even though the basic rule is to hunt facing into it, this isn't always possible. Animal trails or animals within view may go in any direction, and sometimes terrain features create problems. To overcome them, a hunter has to make decisions that may require either taking lengthy detours to avoid getting into a following wind, or if a cover scent is being used, staying on the same course and hoping for the best.

*Several commercial products are available to help hunters judge subtle wind direction. This one is highly visible and biodegradable.*

The worst scenario is a shifting wind that is constantly changing and seems at times to be coming from all directions at once. No matter what tactics are used, the odds are stacked against a stillhunt, but some hunters don't mind long odds.

Animals are also confused by a shifting wind and tend to stay in one place rather than move about. The downside is that without being able to depend on their noses, they're nervous and looking around everywhere for possible danger.

## BAD WEATHER

Stalking bowhunters have their best chances of getting close to deer and other big game during periods of extreme cold, rain or snowstorms. At such times the animals move into cover and bed down. They're less alert because they're relaxed and sometimes asleep, and a stealthy hunter can quite often get to within a few yards of them fairly easily.

This means going out in some really tough weather conditions, but for bowhunters who are looking for new experiences, it represents both an exciting challenge and a chance to take a big-game animal in a different kind of circumstance.

## CLOTHING

The choice of clothing is very important, too, especially when you're passing through shrubs, branches and briars. With garments made of fabrics like brushed cotton, chamois or fleece, you can move more quietly than in those with harder finishes. The sound of a bramble sawing across the surface of

*Top-of-the-line hunting boots are now waterproof, breathable, insulated, and include scent-blocking properties. These boots even have camouflage right down to their soles.*

a regular hunting jacket can be heard for a remarkable distance, and it's one that rings an alarm bell in an animal's mind.

The demand by bowhunters was a principal force in convincing the outdoor industry to create "quiet clothing" that has enhanced the ability to move through cover almost noiselessly. Not surprisingly, it has become extremely popular with gun hunters for the same reasons, so everyone has benefited.

Footwear is another item that deserves consideration. The venerable and famous L.L. Bean Maine Hunting Shoe has been worn by generations of hunters heading afield. These days, there are also boots being made by L.L. Bean and many others that incorporate camouflage designs, improved traction, and comfort with breathable waterproof material, insulation and scent-blocking technology—all wrapped up in a lighter boot. Boots to match virtually any terrain and weather are available in a wide range of styles. Good boots are worth the price, as anyone who spends a lot of time tramping through the woods will attest.

To grant traditional bowhunters their due, it's well to note they believe that Indian moccasins are the quietest footwear in the woods. If that's so, then maybe bare feet are even better!

# KNOWING THE TERRAIN

Knowing what you're doing when stillhunting is one thing, but knowing *where* is quite another, so having as thorough knowledge as possible of the area you'll be stalking is a way to increase your chances of success.

Remember that you're seeking animals on their own turf, so to speak, and within it they have intimate knowledge of all its features. This includes normal travel routes, seasonal feeding and watering locations, places to seek sunshine and warmth on cold days, dense cover for either safety or protection from the weather, the best points from which to observe the most territory, escape routes and all other things that have to do with daily routines and survival.

Your responsibility as a stillhunter is to learn as much about all of these things as you can in order to be able to compete and sometimes to second-guess or anticipate what your adversary is going to do.

There is more than one way to go about gaining this knowledge, the best being to spend as much time as possible scouting the area prior to the season. Preferably, you should do this at different times of the year in order to get a better idea of what the animals are doing seasonally and how their habits vary.

Your scouting forays will familiarize you with the terrain, the animals that live there, where their food is located, where they sleep and the routes of their trails.

You can begin by studying topographic maps and talking with people who know the area. Once you have permission from the landowner your scouting can begin in earnest. Look for open fields, areas of cover, any structures or natural barriers, and water supplies. Pinpointing these features on your map will refresh your memory later.

With the aid of binoculars or a spotting scope, you can study the open fields during early morning and late evening from a distance. Inside the cover, look for trails leading to the fields, heavily traveled trails, and bedding areas.

The ability to read game sign is an important skill that will enable you to identify the places just mentioned. For example, if your quarry is deer, from their tracks you can determine the size of the game, the number of game animals passing through the location, and the direction of their movement.

When you see a rub, or an area of a tree or bush that has been rubbed repeatedly, you can be sure of the presence of a buck in the area. There may be

## STALKING OPEN-COUNTRY GAME
By Judd Cooney
*Pagosa Springs, Colorado*

Mule deer, elk, whitetails and antelope are all animals that originally spent much of their time in open country, but as the population increased, they were forced to adapt to areas of heavier cover and rugged terrain in order to survive.

A bowhunter today often encounters one of these critters that doesn't play according to the rules. Instead, it spends much of its time out in the open where getting within arrow range can seem impossible.

Patience is the bowhunter's greatest asset in open-country stalking. A good set of binoculars is the second most important item in your stalking arsenal, allowing you to study the animal and its surroundings.

I prefer to let the animal come to me if at all possible, or at worst make it a 50-50 proposition: I'm stalking toward it while it is moving toward me. Seldom will stalking along behind an animal put you within bow range. Spend time with your binoculars, determining what the animal is doing and where it is going, and then try to anticipate a course that will put you in front of it and in the best cover possible. This may be a small gully, a single small bush, or a rock outcropping. Avoid large, obvious ambush sites! These animals will walk within a few feet of an unlikely place, but they always seem to stay just out of arrow range of the more obvious places. The bigger the trophy, the sharper the animal.

Always keep the wind in your face and the sun at your back or side, if possible. Animals dislike looking directly into the sun—and if you can stay in a shadowed area, so much the better.

You're probably going to get just one chance to stalk that particular animal in that area. When there is simply no feasible way to approach the animal in open terrain, you must recognize this fact and simply back off and wait for another time.

Stalking to within bow range and making a clean kill on a big-game animal in open country has to be the epitome of the bowhunting experience and the supreme challenge for all bowhunters.

*Expert bowhunter Judd Cooney has been hunting with a bow since 1956. He is a full-time freelance writer/photographer who covers all outdoor subjects, specializing in large-game hunting with bow and gun. He is also an outfitter for Colorado big game. He holds several Pope & Young record-book animals, and until 1990 was tied for the P&Y World Record Antelope.*

a series of rubs going between a bedding area and a feeding area. If some rubs are new and others much older, the area is well traveled, and chances are even better that you may see a buck.

*A variety of scents and calls can help stalking hunters get within shooting distance of game animals.*

Another indicator of both bucks and does is the scrape, an exposed area on the ground that results from pawing. These are made during the breeding season and are usually located under low branches that have been broken by the chewing and rubbing of bucks who want to get the attention of the does.

During most bow seasons the deer are usually very busy eating. They like tender tips of plants, or browse, and a close look will tell you if the plant tips have been torn off. Acorns are a favorite deer food, but many types of field crops and wild plants complete their diet.

You can also learn much by studying the droppings. Different sizes indicate different sizes of animals, and where you see both old and new droppings the area is in use throughout a period of time.

Bedding, or resting, areas are identified by leaves or other ground cover that are matted down. They indicate an area in which the deer will rest. In cold weather they will likely be found in sunny, southern exposures with a minimum of cover.

Finally, look for hair on obstructions along deer trails, such as fences or large fallen logs.

Once you determine the presence of deer and the composition of the population, plan your strategy according to the information you have gained. You may want to ambush a big buck in a bedding area, and so you will become very familiar with the location in order to get on stand while it is still dark. You will also need to identify the trails and the deer's direction of movement. An intersection of trails is also a potential hot location for a stand.

Some of the most successful hunters visit an area many times during the course of a year to observe changes in food sources, population movements, and onset of breeding activity.

While nothing beats this kind of personal investigation and exploration, sometimes you're going on a hunt in a location you haven't visited before. In this kind of situation, having a topographical map well in advance of the trip will give you essential information. Make notes on how the land lies and of some of the features like old logging roads, openings and prominent landmarks that can be used to your benefit.

And don't forget that when hunting in unknown territory, particularly when a large expanse is involved, it's wise to use a compass to plot your course or carry a GPS device. At the least, getting lost in the woods is embarrassing; at worst, it can be extremely dangerous, especially in adverse weather conditions. The little time it takes to prepare yourself this way will make you feel more confident and comfortable and remove the possibility of such things happening.

—

# 9

# DRIVING

Driving is a tactic that is very useful in hunting some kinds of game, particularly deer, and one that often will get results when other methods fail. Driving often works when the animals aren't on the move or are in dense cover that's impossible to stalk successfully; or when weather conditions make other forms of hunting impractical or unproductive. What's more, it's also a useful strategy to consider as an added attraction following a normal morning's hunt in the woods, since it can be a way to put some more venison on the camp meat pole.

Bowhunters conduct drives differently than gun hunters do. The latter generally like to make noise to startle the animals and run them out of their refuges. In bowhunting, the idea is to move slowly and quietly, making the animals aware of the drivers' presence, but not attempting to put them on the run. The reason for this is that a deer that isn't alarmed won't bolt, but instead will try to slip along ahead of the hunter. This way the standers, those at the

## DRIVING DEER
By Paul Butski
*Niagara Falls, New York*

I've been driving deer for a number of years while bowhunting. It's a good activity around midday when you've been sitting in a tree stand all morning, and it's when the deer will be bedding down. A few hunters can get together, put on some "silent drives" and often have good success.

If there are just a few guys, you should look for small patchy woods or good bedding areas where you can hunt effectively. I like to have some good funneling areas for the guys that will be on post. Deer don't like to break out in open areas, so in narrow strips of woods where there are fields outside, they will funnel toward the end. Deer also like to break across a road or on the end of a little draw or in a creek bottom. It takes a bit of scouting to find these escape routes.

To be more successful, learn to read signs in the woods. Improving your woodsmanship will help you to determine those areas deer are moving through.

Bigger bucks like to double back when driven. If there are enough hunters, some can serve as posters, some as drivers, and others as followers 75 to 100 yards behind the drivers to bag those big bucks that double back. A lot of bucks will be off the paths somewhat, so keep your eyes open for deer that try to sneak through that way.

Posters need to get into position quickly and quietly, without being seen by the deer. Otherwise, the animals will move out even before the drivers get there.

Wind is probably the single most important factor in driving deer, whose keenest sense is smell. The drivers should be downwind. There are three basic driving styles: silent drives, noisy drives, and circle drives. In a circle drive, everybody is a driver. The drivers form a circle around a small patch of woods, for example, and then converge at a slow pace. Deer are likely to break toward somebody.

Cornfields are also good places for driving. Drivers can string across the field and work the rows, and often you will see deer standing or lying in there.

I like silent drives best. First, everybody has a chance at getting a deer. Deer can run into the poster or back into the driver, even circle back. The drivers can string out 50 to 75 yards apart and just walk and stop, walk and stop, quietly. The deer may bolt a little, stop, and then start moving again. There are many different driving patterns—crisscrosses, loops and the like—all of which can work effectively.

Noisy drives are not recommended for bowhunters, because it's next to impossible to get anything but a running shot.

One final point: Don't put on a drive if you expect to hunt the same area later that evening. The human scent you bring in will scare the deer away. They'll be back, of course, but maybe not that night.

*Paul Butski, a national turkey-calling champion, is considered one of the top whitetail and turkey hunters in the U.S. In conjunction with his business partner, Billy Macoy, he has produced several highly rated hunting videos. He owns a company that manufactures a variety of game calls.*

*Driving can be an effective hunting technique when deer are laid up in dense cover. Standers must be extremely careful to keep an eye on the position of the drivers at all times.*

end of the woodlot or whatever cover is being driven, don't have to anticipate trying to hit a target that's running wide open.

Successful drives can be organized with as few as two hunters, with one walking through the cover and the other waiting at the end. Four work a lot better, with two driving and two standing. Of course, this can be enlarged to any number desired. Part of this depends upon the size of the area that's going to be driven.

Whatever number of drivers are involved, it's important for them to remain close enough so a deer can't reverse its direction and come back between them. Being within sight of each other is the best rule of thumb to determine this distance.

On short drives it usually isn't necessary to have standers along the flanks, but on long ones there's the distinct possibility that the deer will attempt to make lateral moves to escape. That's one reason why they shouldn't be attempted by a small group of hunters. If there are only two to four involved, pick out spots that can be properly handled.

At times it may be preferable to have the standers actually in elevated stands, since this provides greater visibility and an additional safety measure. Missed shots from stands send arrows into the ground instead of sailing out through the woods.

Driving involves stalking, or stillhunting, skills. The difference is in what you're trying to accomplish. The chances of a driver getting a good shot at a deer are not very good, but sometimes it can happen, as when a deer tries to sneak back through the "enemy lines." Because of this, the hunter has to be prepared, but also fully aware of where both his driving partner and the standers are located. In some cases, the drivers go unarmed, and there's merit in that kind of thinking. Another very sensible suggestion is that drivers all wear some kind of blaze orange, whether it be a vest or a cap.

Something deer hunters sometimes overlook is that both whitetails and blacktails are animals that are likely to be found in small woodlots or other forms of cover close to areas of human habitation, or even near interstate highways where noise is a constant factor. These are places that are particularly well suited for drives, mainly because they are usually ignored by stillhunters or standhunters. Some others with good potential are wooded areas along stream or riverbanks, grown-up thickets in sinkholes or stands of planted pines.

Big-game animals other than deer can be driven, but not as dependably or as successfully, and the methods differ considerably.

Antelope can be manipulated in this fashion to some degree by having a hunter or hunters walk slowly toward them with the hope of causing them to run in the direction of companions already in position and hidden. This can sometimes work with caribou, too, and occasionally with elk, but in each of these cases it's a long-shot proposition and highly unpredictable. Ordinarily there's too much open territory involved and the animals have too many choices of escape routes. Frankly, it's better to hunt them in more traditional ways.

# 10

# SMALL GAME

Bowhunters sometimes get caught up in thinking about big game, but they shouldn't lose sight of the pure fun and satisfaction that hunting small game can provide. It's a form of the sport in which individuals of all ages and levels of experience can participate, and not infrequently the hunt can begin as close as your own backyard. Too, licenses for small-game hunting are less expensive than those that include big game. Some states even allow certain small-game species to be hunted without any license requirements at all.

There's another big advantage, which is that the accuracy required to bring down small targets makes this activity very beneficial, providing an excellent way to hone shooting skills. It is an ideal training ground for young bowhunters, and it is an extremely important activity for veteran shooters.

There are many kinds of small animals to choose from, but the favorite by far is the rabbit. One or more kinds of rabbits are found all over North America. There are more than a dozen species, but the most common are the

---

**SMALL-GAME HUNTING**
By Richard "Rick" Sapp
*Gainesville, Florida*

Small-game hunting is the undiscovered country of archery: squirrel, rabbit, hare, pheasant, groundhogs, prairie dogs, raccoon, red fox, rough fish and more. Not an endless list, but it is long and the populations are generally healthy from coast to coast.

Hunting small game with the bow and arrow does not require an investment in clothing or gear beyond what you have acquired for hunting deer. You may wish to alter your shooting style, however, to shoot quicker at smaller, faster targets:

- by lightening the draw weight of your compound bow or even switching to a recurve,
- by dismounting your sights and shooting instinctively,
- by shooting with fingers rather than a release aid.

Although your basic deer hunting equipment will serve your needs very adequately for small game, you may wish to acquire a few additional accessories:

- small-game heads such as blunts or Judo Points for your arrows,
- flu-flu arrows with wide, fluffy fletching to reduce their flight distance,
- heavy-duty brush trousers or leggings, since you may often find yourself moving through thick ground cover (and in certain areas of the country, leggings to prevent snakebite are advisable),
- a variety of game calls for squirrels, fox, crows, coyotes or turkeys,
- a belt bow carrier which will leave your hands free for binoculars, when moving through cover, or when you need to assist your children in some way,
- bowfishing reels, arrows and harpoon heads,
- a backpack and canteen for a long, beautiful day wandering afield (and it's a place to carry your small-game trophies, too).

*Richard Sapp, director of advertising for Bear Archery, Inc., has been bowhunting since the mid-1970s. He has hunted caribou, pronghorn antelope and black bear and has several antelope and bear in the Pope & Young record book.*

---

cottontails—eastern, swamp, marsh, mountain and desert—and the whitetail and blacktail jackrabbits.

Bowhunters also like to hunt snowshoe hares. They're found throughout Canada and Alaska, but in the U.S. they're limited mainly to New England, the Northwest, the Rockies and some midwestern states bordering Canada.

Hunting rabbits with a bow is a stalking game, and while it can be done solo, it's something in which several people can be involved. Three or four hunters conducting rabbit drives through cover patches can usually come up with some tasty game dinners.

Keen eyesight is a bowhunter's best advantage when hunting rabbits, because spotting them before they bolt permits a chance for a shot at a stationary target. Once a rabbit is flushed and on the move, the chances of hitting it are sharply diminished. One key is to look for the rabbit's eye rather than the entire form. It's the only part of its body that isn't camouflaged, and once you develop this skill, it can make a big difference in what you bring home.

This kind of hunting allows the hunter to use a light bow. Shots will be at close range, and only minimal weight is required. Most cottontails can be successfully taken with blunts that deliver sufficient shocking power to knock them down. For the larger swamp and snowshoe rabbits, though, broadheads are a better choice. The same goes for the big, tough jackrabbits.

There are myriad kinds of both tree and ground squirrels in North America, the majority of which provide the bowhunter only with small, challenging targets. However, the eastern gray squirrel and the eastern fox squirrel are prized for their table qualities as well. Both species occupy almost every state from the Great Plains to the Atlantic Ocean, the exception being that the fox squirrel isn't found in upper New England.

Gray and fox squirrels have traditionally been the favorite quarry of small-game hunters, and in earlier days they were an important source of food for rural families. Almost every farm boy had an all-purpose dog that would

*Small game like the snowshoe hare (left) and jackrabbit (right) can offer bowhunters some challenging shooting at small targets.*

tree squirrels or go after any other kind of game. In those days a single-shot .22 rifle was the standard weapon, but now there is a new generation of hunters who enjoy the challenge of seeking these sly and elusive animals with a bow.

As mentioned in an earlier section, stalking skill is essential for success in squirrel hunting, but so is the bowhunter's ability to shoot accurately. Squirrels are lean and long and present a pretty small target, regardless of the range. That makes getting as close as possible very important. A light bow and either blunt or field points are the best combination.

One species that can be both exciting and sometimes a bit risky is the javelina, or peccary, of the Southwest. These little wild pigs have nasty tempers and tough hides, and they're formidable adversaries for bowhunters. They ordinarily run in packs and aren't easily intimidated. On many occasions hunters have been charged and put up trees by the ornery critters. This is an animal that should be hunted with a bow in the 45- to 60-pound range, and with razor-sharp broadheads.

If a bowhunter wants to do a little night shooting, raccoons and opossums can offer some fun and excitement. Hunting with dogs is the best and surest way of locating and treeing these animals, although in the fall opossums can often be found easily by visiting some persimmon trees and spotting them with a flashlight. For some hunters, bagging these animals is all that counts, but others like to eat them.

*Raccoons make interesting small-game targets, as they are quick and usually hunted at night.*

Speaking of nocturnal activities, the sport of hunting bullfrogs shouldn't be overlooked, because these amphibians are challenging targets for bowhunters and a source of some fine eating. A platter of frog legs is a real delicacy! Bullfrogs are widely distributed. Farm ponds are favorite spots. Lakes, bayous, swamps, canals, irrigation ditches, and stream- and riverbanks are also good prospects. Usually there's no problem getting permission to hunt farm ponds, especially if you explain that you'll share the bounty.

It's possible to hunt frogs solo by using one of the variety of headlights that permit both hands to be free, but it's much more effective when done as a two-man team. That way the light can be more steadily directed, and if you're both bowhunters you can double the fun by taking turns shooting.

Some kinds of frog territory can be hunted effectively only by wading, but in other places a canoe or light aluminum flat-bottom boat is necessary. The main thing is to move as quietly as possible, because frogs are extremely shy. Any loud or unusual sound will cause them to submerge and disappear.

A light bow is sufficient to use for frogs, and arrows with three-pronged gig-type points are the best.

Some states have seasons and limits on bullfrogs, so it's wise to check out your local regulations before planning a hunt.

# 11

# THE KING AND OTHER BIRDS

Not too many years ago the goal of most bowhunters was to bag some kind of big game, because it was commonly believed that only deer, elk, bears and other large animals could provide the kind of challenge worthy of testing their hunting and shooting skills.

This was before what could be called "the wild turkey revolution" began and caused some enormous changes to take place in the world of bowhunting. Once considered as somewhat incidental by archers, turkeys now rank right up at the top in the trophy category and on bowhunters' priority lists. To some, they have become the ultimate trophy.

There's good reason for this changed view of the challenge turkeys offer bowhunters, the proof being that many hunters with impressive records of big-game kills have yet to put an arrow into a gobbler—and this isn't because they haven't tried!

Significant, also, is that because turkey hunting has been such a fast-growing bowhunting sport, it has also had huge ramifications within the archery industry in regard to equipment design innovations.

The challenge of hunting turkeys has always been there, but the astounding rise of this bird to the position of being one of the most sought-after bowhunting prizes is a phenomenon that has much to do with availability.

The enormous increase in turkey populations was brought about by two concurrent practices. Highly successful restocking and restoration programs were introduced in the original turkey range, and at the same time new turkey populations were being developed in places where they had not existed before. In almost all instances, these "exotics" have flourished, and many states that previously had no tradition of turkey hunting can now offer hunters generous seasons and bag limits. The result of the combined efforts is that these magnificent game birds can now be legally hunted in more than three-fourths of the lower forty-eight states. Seasons vary from place to place. Some states have only spring seasons, some only fall dates, and still others allow hunting in both spring and fall.

## TURKEY SPECIES

There are four important subspecies of wild turkey in the United States, one with a range that includes well over half of the country, two with fairly large areas of distribution in the South and West, and another that is found in only one state. Essentially, all are very much alike except for a few minor color variations on the wings and bodies, and some more noticeable differences in the tips of the tail feathers.

The best known and most numerous of these is the eastern variety. Originally, the territory it inhabited extended from Maine to Florida, west to Texas and northward through Nebraska to South Dakota. Since in recent years this subspecies has been used to stock some of the states that were once barren of turkeys, its range has been further extended.

The eastern bird is special in hunters' hearts, because it is the subspecies that contributed the most to the great popularity turkey hunting now enjoys. Nearly all of the calls, calling techniques and hunting tactics were developed hunting them in places like Pennsylvania and the Deep South. Even at the turn of the century when turkey populations had vanished from many states, these places had huntable populations that allowed the sport to remain viable and consequently preserved the tradition. The eastern wild turkey was the one served at the Pilgrims' first Thanksgiving dinner, and it is the species most frequently featured in illustrations.

*The wild turkey is one of the great success stories in wildlife management. Different subspecies are flourishing from New England and the South to the Midwest and West. Their keen eyesight and hearing make them a very difficult target for bowhunters.*

The Rio Grande turkey's home range was from central Texas into Mexico, sometimes overlapping slightly into the eastern bird's range to the north, and into the Merriam's to the west. Like the eastern bird's, the Rio Grande's boundaries have also been widened by transplanting.

The Merriam turkey occupied the most western range of all, which included Colorado, Arizona and parts of northern Mexico. They are now found in states farther north, among them South Dakota, Wyoming, and Montana, and they have adapted well in these places.

The Osceola is native to the Florida peninsula, and it is the only subspecies that has neither migrated nor been the subject of stocking at other locations. There is no reason to do so, mainly because of the abundance and availability of eastern birds for this purpose. The Gould's wild turkey isn't really of concern to American hunters, as almost all of its range lies in Mexico.

## HUNTING TACTICS

All wild turkeys are alert, suspicious, elusive and deceptive. It has been said that wild turkeys exist in a state of constant nervousness, and anyone who has hunted them will agree to that.

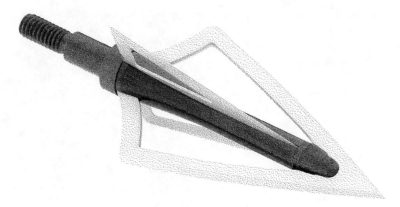

*Broadheads that cut on contact and make wide entry holes are popular with turkey hunters.*

One of the birds' most valuable assets is uncanny vision. The eye of a turkey may appear to be small and somewhat beady, but in reality the eyeball is quite large, with the capacity of much greater resolution than a human eye. In a sense, it could be compared with an extreme wide-angle camera lens, because it has enormous peripheral vision that comes close to allowing it to see to the rear.

Another thing: When looking around, a person's eye focuses on one object at a time. A turkey's eye, however, apparently focuses on *everything* at once. This "all-seeing" capability allows it to detect even the slightest movement. When veteran hunters declare that a wise old gobbler can spot the blink of an eye at 40 yards, it's a statement that's hard to argue, especially if you've had personal experience with the birds.

Because of this keen eyesight, it's vital that a hunter be as nearly invisible as possible. This means not only total camouflage from head to toe, but also for the bow, arrows and other accessories. This is one particular area in which the bowhunter is disadvantaged over a gun hunter, because the latter can remain immobile up until the trigger is pulled. Being camouflaged often requires nothing more than breaking up the human outline. When a hunter wears camouflage, it isn't a person the turkey sees. What catches its eye is an *object* that doesn't belong in the scene. Just being camouflaged isn't sufficient for a bowhunter, because at some point the bow must be drawn. That means motion, and unless the hunter is thoroughly concealed, it's almost a sure thing

## BOWHUNTING BLINDS: PROS AND CONS
### By Richard Combs
#### Cincinnati, Ohio

One of the primary challenges of hunting turkeys with a bow is drawing the bow without being spotted. The bowhunter who hunts without a blind must be prepared to bring in a lot of gobblers before getting a decent shot at one. By contrast, the bowhunter who brings a gobbler into range while concealed in a blind can usually get off a good shot.

Apart from the huge advantage of being able to get shots at unalerted gobblers, over the years I couldn't help abut notice a few other things that greatly reduced my frustration with blinds. First, I noticed that my lack of mobility did not decrease the number of turkeys I saw or got within range of. In fact, if I was hunting with another hunter, I saw more turkeys from a blind, assuming I was hunting an area I had scouted or was familiar with. While I missed traveling light and being highly mobile, the notion that being free to chase and set up on numerous gobblers all over the woods will result in seeing more turkeys is, in the long run, an illusion. The hunter who is familiar enough with an area to know where the turkeys are going to strut, feed, dust, or rest, or which ridgelines, logging road, trails, or other routes they are going to use in traveling between these areas, can see many or more turkeys be setting up in these areas as by chasing gobblers through the woods and setting up on them. They can also do it without disturbing birds and decreasing gobbling activity or changing other patterns.

Then, too, I began to appreciate the unique advantage of a blind. If I gave up some freedom and mobility, I gained comfort and relaxation. I could move in a blind, even with a tom in sight. I could scratch where it itched, knock a bug off my face, change positions. I could even stand up and stretch in some blinds. There are less pleasant ways to spend a spring morning than sitting comfortably.

The perfect blind has yet to be invented; all involve trade-offs of one sort or another. The lightest ones are apt to move in the wind, which can spook turkeys. The blinds that are less likely to flap in the wind are more likely to be heavy, or may require a little more time to set up. Some blind materials are quieter than others. There is the issue of durability. Cost is always a factor, and as you might expect, the best blinds are usually among the more expensive.

Blinds do not guarantee success, of course, but they do offer advantages, especially for the bowhunter. It can almost feel like cheating to have a gobbler approach the blind in complete confidence as you shift position, sip coffee, change calls, get your bow in position, and draw, without being seen.

*Richard Combs has written a number of important books on turkey hunting, and is a recognized expert in the field. He is currently working on a new book,* Turkey Hunting Tactics of the Pros, *to be published by The Lyons Press later this year.*

Full camouflage is a necessity for anyone serious about pursuing wild turkeys.

that the bird will notice. That's why it's critical that particular attention be paid to the blind.

There are several options. Some light, portable, easily assembled blinds specially designed to meet bowhunters' needs are on the market. Camouflage netting can be used to construct very satisfactory blinds, and occasionally natural features like blowdowns, depressions in the ground, or small patches of cover can be made to work okay with just a few changes and adjustments.

The late Ben Rodgers Lee always maintained that successful turkey hunting consisted of 80 percent woodsmanship and 20 percent calling, and he said he wasn't entirely sure that a 90 percent to 10 percent ratio might not be a better estimate. Since Ben was a world champion turkey caller and probably the best and most versatile turkey hunter of all time, his words are worth some thought.

The woodsmanship part is particularly important in this case, since without the skills described in the chapter on stalking, your chances of bringing home a bird are slim. It's essential that you have a good knowledge of turkeys and their habits: how they behave seasonally, their food preferences, and their general routes of travel. You should also be able to identify turkey signs in the woods and locate roosting sites. All this requires pre-season scouting and a lot of watching and listening. You don't just go into unfamiliar territory on opening day and start wandering around.

Calling is not only an important aspect of turkey hunting but also a skill that once perfected becomes a matter of personal pride. It's true that sometimes even the most basic and amateurish calling can be productive, but this is an exception that should be disregarded. The goal is to be consistently successful, and this takes practice and dedication.

In the spring, calling is the most important tool a hunter can possess for locating gobblers, getting their attention and luring them within range. The toms are trying to assemble harems, and hen yelps are the calls to which they are most likely to respond. However, if the gobbler already has a fairly large entourage of lady turkeys, convincing him he needs another can be very difficult. Yet this is what part of the challenge is all about, and what adds the electricity a hunter feels throughout the tense battle of wits and—figuratively speaking—words.

Calling works in the fall, also, but it is done differently and doesn't involve the gobbler-hen drama experienced in the spring. During this season, the old males generally travel together away from the hens and young jakes. The tactic that works best is to find a flock, run in and scatter them, then try to call them back in. They have the desire to be together and are eager to regroup.

The first hunters probably used their own voices to imitate turkey calls, and while some individuals still can do this, it's seldom practiced. Besides, it isn't necessary anymore. Virtually every kind of turkey call ever devised by man is available commercially, and these range all the way from ones that require little or no experience to those preferred by the experts. The difference is usually in the versatility and quality of sound that is made possible by the call.

## TYPES OF CALLS

Basically, there are two kinds: friction calls and mouth calls. The former include the traditional box calls, ones that use wood or plastic strikers scraped across slate or aluminum, hand-cranked devices that produces yelps, a spring-loaded call that can be operated with one hand, and many other variations.

*Box calls are very popular among beginners and advanced turkey callers, as they are reliable and easy to use. A strap to secure the top against making noise while moving is a good idea.*

The classic wing-bone call is an example of a mouth call. Sound is produced by sucking air in rather than expelling it. The tube type consists of a piece of thin surgical rubber stretched over a plastic cylinder, with sound created by holding the call against the lips, exhaling and causing the rubber to vibrate.

The small diaphragm call held inside the mouth is the favorite of bowhunters because it allows them to have both hands free at critical moments. It's a simple device: a piece of thin rubber in a U-shaped plastic or aluminum frame. The call is held against the palate with the tongue and sound is produced by a controlled breath release. The diaphragm call is more than practical, though: it's also the choice of experts. No other call can produce such a wide variety of turkey sounds, or ones that are as authentic.

When trying to get a response from a gobbler, especially in the spring, there are sounds other than "turkey talk" that are effective. A tom with mating on his mind is so excited and aggressive that he regards almost any kind of sound or noise as a challenge. Thunderclaps will sometimes do it, as will slammed car doors or train whistles.

These aren't things that can be depended upon, or made to happen at will. It's better to have one or more of the different kinds of game calls in your

*The diaphragm call is held in the mouth, leaving both hands free. It's a type favored by many hunters, particularly when a bird is approaching.*

*There are many different kinds of turkey calls available, but all fall into two basic categories: those operated by mouth and friction calls operated by hand.*

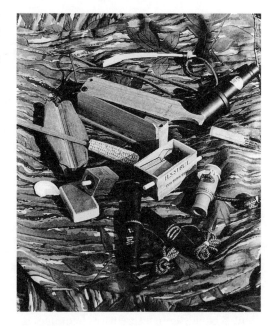

arsenal. These create sounds that are normally heard in the woods and aren't alarming, but which will still get a red-hot gobbler to reply. The best known and probably the most used of these is the owl-hooter, which duplicates the cry of the barred owl. Many hunters can produce this vocally, but there are also several commercial models that do it equally well. A crow call is a good choice, and hawk calls often get results when other kinds fail.

## EQUIPMENT AND SHOOTING

While any bow of legal draw weight can be considered as adequate for turkeys, in the tense situations encountered by a turkey hunter where movement is such a critical factor, compound bows have one particular and very important advantage over stick bows: they permit a hunter to anticipate the right time to shoot and then to draw and hold until the moment arrives. This provides a grace period of several extra seconds that wouldn't be possible using other types of bows. Compound bows of lighter weight and a high degree of let-off make it easier to hold a draw for a longer period of time, but there are other things that deserve consideration. A heavier-weight bow will deliver an arrow faster with a flatter trajectory, giving the bird less chance to react to either the motion or sound. Also, the greater stored energy will deliver more shocking power. A large broadhead with at least three blades, along with one of the devices that attach to the arrow behind the point to keep it from passing entirely through the bird, are advantages. The big broadhead will do a lot of internal damage, and it's more difficult for a gobbler to fly or run with an arrow in its body. Turkeys are as hard to kill as they are to hunt, so don't underestimate this.

Of all the species included in the big-game category, none offers a greater challenge to a bowhunter's shooting ability than the wild turkey. Size is the reason, of course. The entire body of a gobbler without feathers is no larger than that of the vital kill zone on the chest of a whitetail deer. Yet beyond that, the upper chest area on a gobbler into which a lethal arrow shot must be placed is only about the size of a grapefruit. The only other deadly possibilities are shots to the neck and head, which are even smaller targets.

This means a bowhunter must be capable of delivering arrows with pinpoint accuracy from a variety of shooting positions and under conditions that are usually far short of ideal. Developing this skill requires a lot of practice, and the best way to become proficient is to do it in places that match field conditions as closely as possible. Shoot from a blind, and from many different kneeling and standing positions. There are three-dimensional turkey targets that are ideal for this, since they can be arranged so as to provide head-on, profile or angled views.

If a turkey is shot and flies or runs, keep it in sight as long as you can and go after it right away. A lethally shot gobbler will sometimes fly 100 to 150 yards before dying, but if you aren't sure where it went, you can still lose it. Turkeys are extremely hard to spot in the woods because of their natural camouflage.

## ACCESSORIES

Specially designed turkey hunting vests are available to accommodate all of the items bowhunters need, and the array of things that can be packed along are too numerous to mention. The important ones are the various calls, insect repellent, compact binoculars, a rangefinder, basic repair and replacement items, and a blaze orange vest or hat to wear when departing the woods, with or without game. Many states don't require these while hunting, but for safety's sake they should be worn at all other times.

## OTHER GAME BIRDS

If all game birds flushed and flew like ringneck pheasants, more bowhunters would be likely to get involved in wingshooting.

This noble pheasant is big, showy and predictable, and bowhunters who pursue them have a commendably high rate of success. Ringnecks occupy open country, and hunters can usually depend upon having them burst into flight at close ranges, particularly if a dog is being used.

Ringnecks are exotic birds that were introduced into this country many years ago, and eventually adapted successfully from coast to coast in many of the northern U.S. states and the Canadian provinces. They're the favorite game bird of many hunters, and in several states of the Midwest and West big populations exist that not only provide great hunting for residents but also attract plenty of nonresidents from states that don't offer this kind of opportunity. Several places in the western states provide some really challenging wing-shooting for species like sharp-tailed grouse, sage grouse, greater and lesser prairie chickens, gray partridge, and blue grouse.

*A flying pheasant is an extremely difficult target for bowhunters to hit without a lot of practice and a little luck.*

*Ruffed grouse (left), blue grouse, and spruce grouse (right) make easy targets for bowhunters in the West, as they show little fear of humans. Many early-season bowhunters have a shot at a "fool hen" dinner while chasing elk in the mountains.*

Not all of the birds available are tough targets. There are some easy pickings for spruce grouse all across Canada. This is a bird that can be taken without wingshooting, because they can be approached to within very close range as they perch on limbs. They have the nickname "fool hen," which is indeed appropriate. Oddly enough, the ruffed grouse, which in its U.S. range is considered one of the most wily of game birds, often exhibits the same kind of indifference in the Canadian woods and can be shot while it is sitting.

*Sage grouse are the largest North American grouse, but that doesn't make them any easier to hit on the wing. Even one bird is a nice trophy for a bowhunter.*

Wingshooting waterfowl doesn't have a large following among bowhunters, but some of the species like Canada geese are big enough targets to be tempting. Also, while duck populations are shrinking in most of the flyways, both Canada geese and snow geese are on the increase. Hunting them over decoys or pass shooting can be great sport for a bowhunter, and next to wild turkeys they're the toughest of all birds to bring down. Also, like gobblers, it takes a well-placed arrow to bring them down.

It must be remembered that these are migratory birds regulated by the U.S. Fish and Wildlife Service, and a federal stamp is required to hunt them. In many places, state waterfowl stamps are required in addition.

Often it's not necessary to make lengthy treks to get the chance to hunt ringneck pheasants and other kinds of large game birds such as wild turkeys and mallards, because all across the nation there are commercial hunting preserves that feature one or all of these species. The preserve system is a boon to hunters who want convenient access to assured action and either lengthy or year-round seasons. They have other benefits, too. They're excellent places to train young hunters, and they also offer elderly hunters an opportunity to enjoy time afield without too much exertion. Finally, they're ideal spots for professional people who have limited time to hunt.

## WINGSHOOTING

Wingshooting may at first appear to be extremely difficult, but it's a skill that most bowhunters can develop with a little practice. There's really nothing mysterious about it. Part of it is based on instincts and how to react to them.

A simple way to get the idea is to pick out a moving object and quickly point your finger at it. You'll find that you're almost always right on target. Now do the same thing with a bow in your hand and you'll most likely discover the same thing. If the object was stationary, your eye would automatically mark the spot and your shot could follow through, but where motion is involved, your point of aim is where you anticipate the object will be seconds later.

Instinctive shooting, snap shooting and other aiming practices were talked about earlier, and individuals learning to wingshoot will have to discover which of these is the most suitable and comfortable. Once perfected, wingshooting becomes second nature in the same way it does for shotgunners. Practicing wingshooting can be done in the backyard with flu-flu arrows of the

*Wingshooting practice with objects like paper plates or Frisbees thrown into the air can help develop the skills needed for instinctive shooting.*

kind used for hunting. These heavily fletched arrows accelerate rapidly enough to be potent for game at short ranges, but they also lose velocity quickly. Because of this they're both safer and easier to find.

There are several options for targets on which to practice. One of the best is some form of the well-known Frisbee, since it can be effectively tossed either vertically or from angles. Some use targets made from corrugated pasteboard or Styrofoam plates, and while these work okay, unless several layers are glued together they're not as easy to throw. Black or red dots or bullseyes can be painted on these targets to establish a precise point of aim.

Some bowhunters who wish to go a few steps further in honing their wingshooting skills use the devices that throw clay pigeons. Some of these can be adjusted in order to better simulate the actual speed of a flushing or passing bird.

As in all shooting sports, there are true experts who accomplish feats almost beyond the imagination, and there are exhibition archers who are able to consistently hit objects as small as aspirin tablets tossed into the air.

*Picking out a single bird to target can be difficult for bowhunters when a huge flock of Canada geese takes flight.*

Realistically, though, most bowhunters will be satisfied with being able to pick off a ringneck!

A medium-weight bow is fine for wingshooting. For hunting pheasants and grouse, some bowhunters use broadheads, but there are bird points made specially for this purpose that also work very well. Field points are all right for practice, but they aren't really satisfactory for downing game birds. In most cases, more than simple penetration is required to an adequate job, and if wild turkeys or geese are being shot on the wing, bigger, multi-bladed points are necessary.

# 12

# VARMINTS

The term "varmint" isn't as easy to define today as it once was. Many of the creatures formerly considered as predators or simply undesirable were legal to hunt year-round without limits or restrictions. Now some of these are either fully or partially protected in many states.

There are some interesting examples of the changes that have occurred. For instance, not too many years ago black bears were classed as varmints rather than game animals in some locations. It also wasn't long ago that hawks, owls and even eagles were fair game for varmint hunters throughout most of their ranges. Shooting any kind of turtle or snake was okay, too, yet many reptiles and amphibians now occupy places on the protected lists in some areas.

Even with some species eliminated from the overall picture, bowhunters shouldn't be dismayed. There are still plenty of opportunities remaining. In fact, one species has increased in numbers so dramatically that no varmint hunter anywhere in the country can complain.

If you haven't guessed already, it's the coyote.

*Coyote*

These animals were once mainly inhabitants of the Southwest, but in the last couple of decades they have migrated outward in all directions. This movement has been so extensive that they are present in every state in the nation, and most Canadian provinces as well. Studies show that some eastern states now have coyote densities that surpass those in the West where they have been present for centuries.

In many ways, the wily coyote could be classed as the king of the varmints. It is intelligent, crafty, fast, tough and best of all from a varmint hunter's standpoint, numerous. You may be under the impression that there are no coyotes in your vicinity, but a little investigation will prove you wrong. Not only are they prevalent in rural areas, but they have become well established in the suburbs, where they raid garbage cans, kill domestic dogs and cats—and on rare occasions small children.

Hunting coyotes is mainly a calling-and-waiting game. Because of their keen senses, stalking these animals is all but impossible. They don't use regular routes of travel like deer, so sitting and waiting for them to appear doesn't work, either. However, they're suckers for the distress calls of rabbits and other small-game species on which they prey. If they get the idea there's a free meal to be had, they can't resist coming after it.

*Red fox*

They also will respond to calls that imitate sounds of their own young being molested, especially if some red fox calls are included to make this animal the villain. There are many other options, because the coyote has an enormous curiosity and can be lured with a wide variety of bird and animal calls.

Since the advent of turkey decoys, it's been discovered that these are very effective coyote attractors. The animals investigate the calls, and the decoys convince them. Since hunters have learned this, the tactics have become a part of their bag of tricks for hunting coyotes at other times of the year.

Another strategy that works well with coyotes is to use fawn decoys at the times when deer are bearing their young. These infant animals are so desirable that upon spotting the decoys, coyotes often abandon all of their normal caution and rush headlong at what they think is an easy target.

Operating from a blind that offers good concealment is important, and for bowhunters a two-man team works best, with one person calling and the other doing the shooting. Coyotes are cautious and almost always circle the spot before coming in. There's no way to know from which direction they'll approach, so having two pairs of eyes scanning is a big advantage. In addition, this permits the caller to continue to coax the animal in while the shooter draws.

Night hunting for coyotes and other varmints was very popular at one time, but this form of the sport has been eliminated in those states that have spotlight laws designed to reduce deer poaching. The law is needed, but it's unfortunate that varmint hunters are restricted because of it.

Red and gray foxes can also be enticed by calls. Their habits and general behavior are very similar to those of the coyote, and long before the expansion of the coyote population in the East, these animals were favorites of varmint hunters. Mouse squeakers and bird and rabbit distress calls are the best for luring these artful predators. There are seasons on foxes in some states, but in a few places where traditional hunting with hounds is conducted, the red fox is protected.

The other large-size varmint that offers bowhunters widespread potential is the bobcat. Some states have now adopted seasons on them, though in almost all cases these are generous in length. So there's still plenty of opportunity throughout this animal's broad range.

*Bobcat*

Bobcats respond to many of the calling tactics that are used for coyotes, and in areas where both are present it isn't unusual to have them show up almost as often. They're sometimes more aggressive than coyotes, which is evidenced by a few instances where bobcats actually pounced on hunters while they were calling.

Groundhogs occupy a large area of North America that encompasses most of the eastern United States, except for parts of the Deep South, and they are in most Canadian provinces and eastern Alaska. These animals, often called woodchucks, are special favorites of varmint hunters because they're numerous and are regarded by most landowners as pests. They do economic damage to crops, and their holes are a hazard to livestock.

Rifle hunters pick off groundhogs at long ranges, but bowhunters must employ careful stalking tactics to get close enough to these burrowers to get off a shot. They're fond of open fields, which makes an approach all the more difficult, so hunting them is excellent practice in stealth and patience.

In the northern states, groundhogs hibernate during the winter, but in the southern states where the climate is more moderate, they merely estivate, emerging whenever there's a nice, sunny day. The prime time to go after

*Groundhog*

groundhogs is in the spring when crops like soybeans are attaining 6 to 8 inches in height. At this time they're out of their dens and foraging, and by watching a field where dens are known to be, it's fairly simple to spot them moving around. Such greenery is like manna to these rodents. Even if the crop isn't in the place where they have their burrows, they will sometimes travel fairly long distances to take advantage of the bounty.

Another animal that's a bonus for bowhunters has emerged on the scene, and that is the beaver. The widespread increase in the beaver populations and the damage they are causing to bottomland timber and small waterways have put them in the varmint category in many states. These are tough critters that can weigh more than 50 pounds, and it takes plenty of power and a good broadhead to kill them. Wounded beavers seldom can be retrieved, since they dive and usually end up in a den that's all but impenetrable. For that reason, make sure when you're placing a shot that it will be lethal.

In the West, the varmint that offers the bowhunter the most opportunity is the prairie dog. It's a much smaller target than a groundhog, and because these animals live in colonies, they're more difficult to stalk. Lots of eyes are watching all of the time. There are also several types of gophers in this region, many of which are legal to take.

*Beaver*

*Prairie dog*

While not necessarily high profile on the varmint list, there are places where skunks, porcupines, armadillos and badgers are plentiful and shouldn't be overlooked as possibilities for some extra shooting action.

Some bowhunters go after crows, because by calling them in to decoys there's the chance to get shots at them both perching and flying. Angry crows often can be brought to within a dozen or so yards and provide some exciting wingshooting. There is another enormous shooting opportunity available in the millions of starlings that blanket fields and lawns almost everywhere in the country. They're challenging targets for shooters who want to achieve pin-point accuracy.

One of the biggest benefits offered by varmint hunting is that it provides the bowhunter with the chance to hunt and shoot at times of the year when the seasons are closed on other species. Regardless of what part of the nation you live in, there are some kinds of varmints, large or small, that can be sought. It's just a matter of checking your state's hunting regulations to determine what's legal and when.

# 13

# FISH

Bowfishing is another sport that broadens the archer's horizon of opportunity, and there are times when it can provide all of the action a bowhunter can handle.

A good example of this occurs in the spring when carp are spawning, or "shoaling" as it's also called. Large numbers of them move into shallow water and mill around. The result is a bonanza for bowhunters.

This might seem like shooting fish in a barrel, but it isn't that easy. A fish in a barrel can't go anywhere, but a big carp may head for parts unknown when it's hit with an arrow. Bowhunters often like to pick out the biggest fish to shoot, and since carp often attain weights of well over 20 pounds, they can get up a pretty powerful head of steam in a hurry!

That's why there's special equipment made for bowfishing that uses the harpoon gun principle. A reel attached to the bow is loaded with heavy fishing line, which is tied to the arrow. When a fish is hit and runs, the line plays out

## BOWFISHING—FUN AND FAST ACTION
### By Deano Farkas
*Easton, Pennsylvania*

Bowfishing can make you a better bowhunter for both big and small game.

Equipment is simple and inexpensive. Any bow will do, though I prefer one in the 60-pound class to handle the heavy fish arrow.

Use solid fiberglass or fish-getter-type aluminum arrows weighing approximately 1,500 grains. Heavy arrows will penetrate any rough fish in 6 to 8 feet of water. I remove the rubber fletch from my bow for better accuracy, because bent rubber fletching may re-steer the arrow in the water.

As to reels, I prefer a spincast Zebco 808 when the fish are "hot and heavy." For large fish, 25 pounds or more, my choice is a simple hand-wind. Always remember safety. Press that button, and keep the line clear of your fingers and equipment.

My fish line is heavy, 90- to 120-pound braided. It is easy to handle and there is less chance of getting cut when you are fighting large fish. Also, a heavy line helps when you are trying to retrieve an arrow from the muck or tangled weeds. Always fasten the line to the rear of the fish arrow. If you fasten it to the front or tip, the shaft will fly sideways and you'll have poor penetration.

Use points with screw-on fronts. Arrows stuck in creek bottoms or logs can be removed easily by turning off the point. Carry extra front ends to replace any lost or dull points. Attach the points to shafts with 24-hour or 2-ton epoxy to give them better shock strength. I pin all my fish points to the shaft by drilling a small hole through the point and shaft and inserting a fine aluminum or brass nail, cut to length.

Scout for pathways through lily pads and weed beds. You can set up ambushes in these fish runs. Smoke trails (mud slicks) will also tell you fish are working in an area. Walk lightly so that carp resting or feeding near the bank will not dash to the middle of the river. And watch the sun position to avoid casting shadows on the water.

Most important: Know and obey the fish and game laws covering the rough fish species in your area.

*Deano Farkas has been bowhunting seriously since 1961 and has hunted in 35 states and 6 Canadian provinces. He has taken over 250 big-game animals of many species, including 28 black bears, and numerous fish and small game. Several animals are in the Pope & Young record book. The largest fish was a 10-foot tiger shark that weighed 265 pounds. Deano has the ABC National Bow Record for a bow-taken turkey, has two Silver Broadhead awards from the NRA, and was named Bowhunter of the Year by Spector Bowhunters in 1981. He is a consultant to industry, a field editor for* Bowhunting World, *and active in 35 outdoor and bowhunting organizations.*

and the fish can be retrieved by either pulling or reeling it in or following it to where it stopped or died.

Another method that works well when shooting from a boat is to take along a rod and reel. Tie the line to the arrow, then remove 15 to 20 yards of line from the reel and coil it away from your feet in the bottom of the boat. When the fish is shot, you'll have enough time to lay down the bow, pick up the rod and be ready to play the fish.

Solid fiberglass arrows are favored for bowfishing, not only because of their toughness, but also since their weight makes it possible for them to be driven deeper into the water than wood, hollow glass or aluminum shafts. Rubber vanes that slip onto the arrow shaft are the most practical kind of fletching.

There are many point designs that work well for bowhunting fish, and either personal experience or professional advice can help to determine which you should use.

One nice thing about bowfishing is that the equipment isn't costly. Usually you can use your regular hunting bow; then it's simply a matter of getting a reel, a couple of arrows and some points.

Besides carp, there are many other types of fish bowhunters can seek. Streams and rivers in many parts of the country have spawning runs of suckers and buffalo that provide plenty of action. Some kinds are very good to eat. Throughout the southern United States the four species of gar—longnose, shortnose, spotted and alligator—hold great potential for the bowfisherman. These fish are throwbacks to prehistoric times, as their appearance suggests. Gar are slim and almost snakelike in appearance, with long, bony beaks and armor plates of tough scales. They vary considerably in size. The shortnose

*A variety of specialized points are available for bowfishers.*

A bowfisherman stands ready to shoot as he and a companion look for shoaling carp.

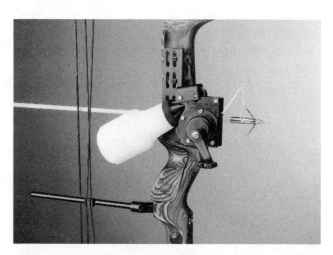

The reel in this bowfishing outfit includes a plastic bottle to stack line instead of the traditional drum, offering less drag as the arrow is released.

and spotted gar seldom exceed 3 feet in length, and the longnose sometimes reaches 5 feet. The alligator gar, however, can become a true giant by freshwater fish standards. Specimens of up to 10 feet in length and 300 pounds have been recorded, and ones in the 6- to 8-foot range aren't uncommon.

Because of their strength and powerful jaws, a hand gaff is recommended to land them, and wearing sturdy gloves is also a good idea. Big alligator gar can be dangerous, since they're very hard to kill and usually aren't mortally wounded by the harpoon arrow. Some individuals use a broadhead to administer the finishing touch, while others prefer a pistol shot to the head as a more positive solution before trying to land them. A 6-foot gar thrashing about in a boat can create havoc!

Gar have a habit of floating just below the surface of the water on hot summer days, and this is an excellent time to go after them. You may see as many as 100 in a school, so there won't be any shortage of action. The bonus gar provide is that they can be hunted throughout most of the year, and often they're present at the same places where carp, sucker and buffalo are found.

Night bowfishing for gar from a boat is also productive, especially for the larger fish. This is a two-man operation, of course, and it requires a powerful spotlight to locate the fish. It helps to have another form of illumination such as a gasoline lantern to provide enough light for shooting.

Wading is an effective method of going after spawning rough fish, whether it be in still or running water. The only problem is that it limits visibility. You can view a much larger area from a boat, and the extra height permits better shooting angles. Some bowfishermen increase this advantage by equipping their boats with high platforms on the bow much like those used by fishermen on saltwater bonefish flats.

*Fiberglass arrows with rubber vanes are still the top choice for bowfishers.*

One item that can be of special benefit to a bowfisherman is a pair of polarized glasses. These help overcome glare that makes it difficult or impossible to see objects underwater.

There's another matter concerning perceiving objects underwater that must be addressed. Because of light refraction, fish aren't where the eye makes them seem to be. Shooting directly at them will result in the arrow passing well above the target. The solution is to aim low. How much you need to compensate depends on how far away the fish is and how deep it is. Trial and error will eventually enable you to be pretty accurate.

Freshwater bowfishermen have no shortage of places to go or species to seek. Almost every body of water of any size will have potential, and usually there are plenty of choices close to where you live. Consider all of the different kinds of rough fish that can be harvested, and you will recognize that there's a bonanza of opportunities.

There's another bonus that shouldn't be overlooked. Carp taken from clean waters are very suitable as table fare, and many people in this country and other parts of the world consider it a delicacy. Its reputation as being undesirable stems from the fact that it is commonly found in polluted waters not inhabited by gamefish. However, it's a different matter when it is occupying suitable habitat.

Gar, on the other hand, are not edible, and they can truly be classed as a nuisance. Shooting them provides bowhunters with a lot of fun, and ridding the waterways of them is a good deed.

The situation in saltwater used to be much the same, but this has changed very much in the last decade. Some species, such as sharks, skates, barracudas and various kinds of rays that were once popular with bowfishermen, are now either illegal to take or regarded as targets that shouldn't be taken. Part of the reason for this is that the populations of some of these fish have been heavily overharvested by commercial fishermen. Also, studies have shown that some, especially sharks, have very slow growth rates and can't replenish themselves fast enough to keep pace with the commercial demand. The stingray remains about the only target bowfishermen can seek legally or without twinges of conscience.

# 14

# FIELD GAMES AND ARCHERY COMPETITIONS

A rchery as a game has a long history. Its beginning was probably as simple as a couple of individuals with bows deciding to find which one could shoot the best. This possibly led to a rematch, or other challenges, and like any activity of this sort, these competitions ultimately became events that followed established rules.

Today archery activities run the gamut from simple backyard or field plinking to the stringent and formal structure of various world-class competitions. In between are the *target* and *field* events—the two major divisions in competitive archery. They are sponsored by various organizations, all of which have their own agendas and rules. There are many variations among these competitions, but in each case a game is called a "round," and an "end" is the number of arrows shot in succession before the score is recorded and arrows are pulled.

Target competition emphasizes the distance to the target, which normally is a round with scoring rings marked in centimeters that determine the score. A deviation of this is a paper target that simulates animal shapes. The round is named for a potentially perfect score, thus a "600 Round" or a "900 Round" game. The end may be from three to six arrows, based on the target's size and distance.

A coveted trophy among target shooters is the Robin Hood, earned by driving the tip and shaft of the arrow deep into the end of another arrow already in the bullseye. Having a Robin Hood—arrows stuck end to end—above one's mantel is considered quite an achievement. It is the archer's "hole in one."

Field events are named for the type of target or the style of approach. Up to four archers, each using his or her distinguishable arrows, may shoot at the same target. Some common events are the Field Round, Hunters' Round and the Animal Round, and it is the latter category that has proved to be the most popular and best received by bowhunters.

The immense increase in interest in bowhunting has been a driving force in bringing many more archers into these activities, especially field archery, since—as was noted in the introduction—so many archers today are

*Hunters can hone their shooting skills on 3-D targets before heading afield.*

*Three-D targets come in a wide variety of styles. Many break down for storage and include a replaceable vitals area.*

bowhunters whose main reason for being involved is to maintain a continuous, year-round practice regimen. Their participation has enhanced archery because it has added special features and events that weren't included traditionally. In the beginning field archery was a close copy of the rifle and handgun game that used animal silhouettes as targets. In the archery version, the targets depict various traditional animals such as chickens, pigs, turkeys and rams that are made of plastic foam rather than metal. Dedicated archers appreciate the additional challenge of having to shoot at groups of three targets from various distances. The first target is a known distance appropriate for the species represented, but the next two force the shooter to estimate the distance. If the arrow topples a target, a hit is declared. A bow with a draw weight of at least 40 pounds is standard for this event, and some competitors use much heavier draw weights that will drop the ram target at 75 yards.

Sometimes these matches are timed events, which require the shooter to get off a large number of arrows very quickly. In such games sighting devices are virtually useless.

This type of competition is excellent for using the compound bow but also offers the opportunity for the barebow archer to practice instinct shooting.

*Virtually every game animal now has a 3-D target, giving hunters a lot of opportunities to practice on realistic targets.*

Some other popular games are Clout, requiring arrows to be lobbed long distances at a single target, and Wand, a relic of an ancient game named for the thin vertical stick of wood that serves as the target.

One of the most significant of the more recent innovations, and the one that's by far the most exciting and authentic, is the three-dimensional, or 3-D, type of competition. These events use solid-bodied, life-size small-game, big-game, bird and varmint targets that must be shot at from unknown distances and a variety of positions, angles and elevations. Bowhunters find them exciting, and they are valuable in keeping both the hunter's shooting skills and the equipment constantly fine-tuned.

One version is called Yukon roving, in which the target is a life-size animal with the vital area marked but only visible at very close range. It is placed either 30 yards away in cover or 40 yards in the open. Each participant has a turn selecting the target location, and sometimes shots must be from a kneeling or leaning position. One shot per round is allowed. A hit in the vital area earns a point while a hit elsewhere on the target deducts two points. No penalty is given for a miss.

Roving is a useful technique for bowhunters that provides field conditions and a variety of shots, depending on the terrain.

In addition to the established organizations, new ones have sprung up in recent years, and both old and new have begun to feature innovative kinds of competitive events that involve forms of shooting and equipment not previously known or sanctioned. New challenges appear continually: variations on timed games; night shoots that feature lighted targets; and shoots with targets that pop up randomly and must be shot at within a matter of seconds.

## ONE BOWHUNTER'S STORY

The story of Rockie Jacobsen of Orofino, Idaho, illustrates how a bowhunter became interested and involved in field games, developed a high degree of skill in competition shooting, and saw that translated into hunting success and fulfillment:

"I began shooting a bow in 1968 at the age of sixteen. My first bow was a Bear recurve. Shooting instinctive was a great challenge and very rewarding. I had some successful hunts, but it was the unsuccessful ones that taught me the most.

"As the years passed, archery became more and more advanced and more popular. In 1973 I switched to a compound bow. It seemed like the thing to do, since it was supposed to be a better way of shooting faster and being

*Other types of targets vary from simple hay bales to high-density foam targets like these.*

more accurate. I could pull more weight and hold less at full draw. This was all achieved by the round wheels put on the compound bow. But I soon found out there was more to archery than just shooting a bow.

"Archery attracted me mainly because of the hunting aspect. In the late 1970s, archery tournaments became very popular, especially 3-D unknown yardages. These 3-D shoots are one of the best ways to help improve your archery skills for hunting. Here you learn to judge yardages, the right angle shots to be taken on animals and how to shoot under pressure. But most of all, it is fun.

"I have been able to win a few local and state shoots and place high in national tournaments. It was in 1990 that I first put together a three-man team and entered the Western Triple Crown archery tournament. My team, consisting of Don West, Tony Hyde and myself, took first place in the open class.

"This type of practice was invaluable. I have taken many different big-game animals such as deer, elk, bear, cougar; and I have hunted grouse, coyote and bobcat. Of all the animals I've taken the greatest thrill was bugling a bull elk to within bow range."

## NAA AND NFAA EVENTS

What has been, and continues to be, important to archery events and the organizations that sponsor them is the preservation of all the traditional forms of equipment and shooting practices. The National Archery Association (NAA) and the National Field Archery Association (NFAA) have done this by closely defining what can and cannot be used in particular events.

The NAA, which is the sponsoring organization for Olympic shooting in the U.S., places great emphasis on excellence on the target line, whereas the NFAA is oriented primarily toward hunting and simulation of actual field shooting situations.

The National Shooting Sports Foundation describes some of the NAA requirements this way:

"In NAA events, most any bow (other than compound) may be used providing it subscribes to the acceptable principle and meaning of the word bow as used in target archery; e.g., an instrument consisting of a handle riser, and two flexible limbs, each ending in a tip with a string nock. The bow is braced for use between the nocks only and in operation is held in one hand by its handle, while the fingers of the other hand draw, hold back and release the string.

Competitions that include 3-D targets, like IBO's World Turkey Championship, have sparked new interest among archers and bowhunters.

Both hunters and competition shooters benefit from good form.

"Arrow rests and an aiming aid such as a bowsight or bowmark are permitted as long as they are not electronic or do not use a lens or a prism for magnification. Stabilizers are also allowed."

These are obviously rules intended for users of traditional equipment such as longbows and recurve bows, so they are necessarily restrictive and prohibitive.

The National Field Archery Association's rules are much broader and are attuned with current archers' preferences, and this has boosted participation by a great many more shooters in recent years.

In NFAA events, equipment is divided into categories: Barebow; Freestyle Barebow; Freestyle; Freestyle Limited Bowhunter; Freestyle Limited; Traditional; Competitive Bowhunter; Freestyle Limited Recurve/Longbow. See their Web site at www.nfaa-archery.org for more information on shooting categories and events.

## OLYMPIC COMPETITION

Olympic archery competition uses the recurve bow. The limbs curve away from the archer to provide increased power. In a lever effect, it propels arrows in excess of 150 miles an hour. These bows are usually of wood, fiberglass and graphite or carbon composites, maximizing the properties of each material. The latest bows are of Syntactic Foam and ceramic, with stabilizers to reduce torque, or twisting, on release; fitted with sights and arrow rests. Most strings are of Fast Flight, a hydrocarbon product; others are of Kevlar, a material used in bulletproof vests. The latter often have "kisser buttons" attached that identify when the archer is at the correct anchor. Arrows are of either aluminum or graphite, with the point, the nock and the fletching attached to the shaft.

Strength is an obvious requirement for an Olympic-class archer. The ancient recurve bow, though made of improved materials and more aerodynamic, is lifted and drawn more than 312 times. With the average draw weight for a man of 50 pounds, that's a total of nearly 8 tons pulled over a four-day period. Women pull nearly 5½ tons with their 34-pound-average bows.

The accuracy required can be likened to standing on the goal line of a football field and hitting an apple under the opposite goal post!

# WORLD TARGET ARCHERY

Internationally, the Fédération Internationale de Tir à l'Arc (FITA), or the International Federation for the Sport of Archery, sets target archery rules for member nations. There are three formats: the Single FITA Round, the Grand FITA Round, and the Olympic Qualification Round.

A Single FITA Round consists of 36 arrows shot from four distances—90, 70, 50 and 30 meters for men; and 70, 60, 50 and 30 meters for women—for a total of 144 arrows. These are fired at bullseye targets. The maximum possible score is 144 "10s" or 1,440 points.

The Grand FITA round starts with a two-day Single FITA of 144 arrows. On the third day, the top 24 male and top 24 female archers play again, with a zero score beginning each new round. Six are eliminated in the morning, and six more in the afternoon. The semifinal round defines the top eight competitors, and the final round determines the medal winners.

The new Olympic FITA Style Competition qualifying round consists of 36 arrows fired from 90, 70, 50 and 30 meters for men and 70, 60, 50 and 30 meters for women. Each archer shoots 12 arrows on a 122-centimeter target at 70 meters. The top 32 women and the top 32 men compete in a single-elimination match play competition until the winners emerge. Team qualification is determined when the first 16 men's and women's teams in the qualification round proceed to the elimination round. In the team competition, 27 arrows (3 by 9) are shot on the target.

# Appendix A

## NATIONAL AND INTERNATIONAL ARCHERY AND BOWHUNTING ORGANIZATIONS

There are quite a few international, national, regional and local archery organizations that provide enthusiasts opportunity for additional involvement in the sport. The national and international organizations described here offer a good starting point for making new friends and promoting interests you feel are important.

### AMERICAN ARCHERY COUNCIL
*604 Forest Avenue*
*Park Rapids, Minnesota 56470*
The AAC is a nonprofit organization that represents virtually all aspects of competitive

archery and bowhunting. There are a number of affiliated organizations with a total membership of more than two million.

**Mission Statement**
The AAC is active in promoting competitive archery and bowhunting, supporting hunter education, and endorsing wildlife management. AAC supports its position through youth education, contributions, legal action, legislative monitoring (state and federal), lobbying, involvement with all outdoor user groups, and cooperative legal intervention on behalf of state bowhunting interests.

**How to Join**
Individuals may join and support one of the affiliated organizations. Direct contributions for specific projects or the AAC general fund may be sent to the American Archery Council Administrative Office (address above).

Contact the AAC Administrative Office for information on programs which raise funds for affiliates. Telephone: 218-732-7747.

### ARCHERY RANGE AND RETAILERS ORGANIZATION
*156 North Main Street, Suite D*
*Oregon, Wisconsin 53575*
*www.archeryretailers.com*

The Archery Range and Retailers Organization is a co-op comprising 140 leading archery pro shops in the USA. The member/stockholders perform as a cooperative buying group. It was incorporated in 1981 and was formerly known as the Archery Lane Operators Association.

**Mission Statement**
The ARRO is a strong group of elite archery retailers that builds consumer confidence by offering low-priced, top-quality archery merchandise.

**How to Join**
Member candidates must be a legitimate retailer and pass rigid screening tests. They must have the highest-rated credit possible; be in a retail location; have been in business for at least three years and have grossed at least $50,000 in each of the past three years. Membership is limited to 500 member/dealers. Telephone: 800-234-7499.

### BOWHUNTERS OF AMERICA
*1025 North 3rd Street*
*Bismarck, North Dakota 58501*
Bowhunters of America (incorporating Bowhunters Who Care) is an organization actively working to protect the continuation of bowhunting in America and defend the sport against detractors. BOA is a member of the AAC, is a North American representative on the World Bowhunting Association Council, and is a major contributor to the Bowhunter Defense Coalition.

Members receive a quarterly magazine, voting rights, and sometimes a chance to win free hunts.

**Mission Statement**
The stated purposes and objectives are: A) to promote and foster fair chase hunting with the bow and arrow; B) to inform and educate bowhunters and the general public by promoting bowhunter education and providing information about the sport; C) to protect and defend bowhunting by assisting local, state and national groups in solving problems pertaining to bowhunting; D) to strengthen bowhunting by working with state and federal wildlife agencies in the wise use of our natural resources and the preservation of our wildlife and its natural habitat; E) to communicate all important bowhunting issues to the people; F) to promote and assist in the solution of environmental and conservation issues on a local, state and national level; G) to assist local and state bowhunting leaders and organizations in resolving legislative issues which adversely affect bowhunting; and H) to promote hunter safety and to promote and defend hunting as a legitimate sport and as a viable and necessary method of fostering the propagation, growth, conservation, and wise use of our renewable natural resources.

**How to Join**
Write BOA at the above address to request a membership application. There are eight levels of membership offered. Telephone: 701-255-1631.

### FRED BEAR SPORTS CLUB
*4600 S.W. 41st Boulevard*
*Gainesville, Florida 32608*
The late Fred Bear, founder of Bear Archery as well as the Fred Bear Sports Club, said: "When civilization reaches the point where its people care nothing for their natural environment, it will cease to exist." Members may be eligible to win awards in the Bowhunting Division of the club, based on applications available at Bear Archery dealers and subject to the Award Approval Committee.

The club also offers a twice-yearly newsletter and free passes to the Fred Bear Archery Museum in Gainesville.

**Mission Statement**
The organization operates under a credo to protect outdoor ecology and support the proper wildlife management of the woods, fields and waters; to uphold the fish and game laws, preserve natural resources and always compete honestly when engaged in outdoor sports. Members also adopt a nine-point "Rules of Fair Chase."

**How to Join**
It is not necessary to be a hunter or an archer to join, and there is no age limit. Contact your local Bear Archery dealer for a membership application, or write the organization directly at the above address.

### INTERNATIONAL BOWFISHING ASSOCIATION
*1049 Crystal Court*
*Lino Lakes, MN 55014*
*www.iba-bowfishing.com*

The IBA is dedicated to protecting, advancing and preserving the sport of bowfishing and its resources, and promoting ethical bowfishing methods. They sponsor events to promote the sport and introduce new archers to this exciting method of bowhunting. Call (651) 653-3279 for membership information.

### INTERNATIONAL BOWHUNTING ORGANIZATION
*P.O. Box 398*
*Vermillion, OH 44089*
*www.ibo.net*
The IBO/USA was created in 1984. The organization is very active in three major areas: bowhunter defense, shooting skill standards, and club insurance.

In the area of bowhunter defense, activities are diverse, and include media coverage, defense funds, lobbying, and support of WLFA and NBEF.

As to shooting skills, IBO promotes standardized shooting rules and classes, provides a national level of competition (the "Triple Crown" of bowhunting, with three national shoots in three different states), and a world level of competition (the annual IBO/USA World Championship, with a series of sanctioned preliminary qualifying shoots in several states and coverage on ESPN). It also promotes scholarships.

The insurance program offers property damage, medical malpractice, and several types of liability coverage to club members.

IBO has helped establish a Bowhunter Week in several

states and has endorsed the National Bowhunter Educational Foundation (NBEF) program that perpetuates our bowhunting heritage.

IBO is part of the WLFA Bowhunting Defense Coalition created to protect the sport nationwide.

**Mission Statement**
IBO was formed to unify bowhunters and bowhunter organizations at an international level for purposes designed to promote, encourage and foster the art and sport of bowhunting, bowhunters' education, act as a liaison for the betterment of bowhunters, function as a clearing house for essential bowhunter information and adhere to the basic ideal of the International Bowhunting Organization/USA, which is the unification of bowhunting.

**How to Join**
Membership is open to individuals, families, and to any club, state organization, or association. Write the IBO at the above address for an application form or to contribute to the Bowhunter Defense Fund. Membership includes a subscription to *International Bowhunter*. Telephone: 440-967-2137.

### INTERNATIONAL FIELD ARCHERY ASSOCIATION
*31 Dengate Circle*
*London, Ontario*
*CANADA N5W 1V7*
*www.archery-ifaa.com*
This is the world's governing body for field archery. Refer to the National Field Archery Association for membership information.

### NATIONAL ARCHERY ASSOCIATION
*One Olympic Plaza*
*Colorado Springs, CO 80909*
*www.usarchery.com*
There are numerous archery organizations in the U.S., but the NAA is the national governing body for national and international competition.

NAA is a "Group A" member of the U.S. Olympic Committee (USOC), which sponsors all U.S. teams traveling to the Olympics and Pan Am Games. It is also a member of the Fédération Internationale de Tir à l'Arc (FITA), the international governing federation for archery. FITA dictates the eligibility requirements and competition rules for international and Olympic archery competition.

The NAA sponsors a number of programs for both beginning and elite archers, students, coaches and officials. The Resident Athlete Program allows archers to live and train full-time at the U.S. Olympic Training Center. The U.S. Archery Team consists of the top eight male and top eight female archers in the country. Team members conduct seminars and are scientifically tested to improve technique, nutrition and physical and mental training. The Junior Elite U.S. Archery Team also has eight top male and eight top female archers under 18. They are given a rigorous training and nutrition program. The Junior Olympic Archery Development (JOAD) program provides—through 175 clubs—archery instruction and tournament activities for thousands of young archers. The NAA conducts training camps for the three categories of archers mentioned. There is also a College Division that has over 45 clubs and intercollegiate teams, and competitions decide the 10 top men and 10 top women each year.

Numerous state archery groups have organized and affiliated with the NAA to bring archery competition closer to the local level and provide yearlong competition geared to the differing age and skill levels of their members.

## Mission Statement

The NAA was formed to foster and promote the sport of archery. It sanctions and conducts tournaments, and chooses the U.S. representatives for international competitions such as those already mentioned, and world championships.

## How to Join

Membership is open to everyone involved in archery, whether as a sport, hobby or craft. One- and three-year memberships are offered for adults, families, youths, full-time students and clubs. Membership includes a free NAA decal, six issues of *The U.S. Archer* magazine, the *NAA Newsletter*, and achievement pins which can be earned at NAA-sanctioned tournaments. To join, write the NAA at the address given above. Telephone: 719-578-4576.

## NATIONAL BOWHUNTER EDUCATION FOUNDATION

*P.O. Box 2007*
*Fond du Lac, Wisconsin 54936*
*www.nbef.org*

The National Bowhunter Education Foundation is a worldwide bowhunting foundation created to protect bowhunting privileges through sportsman education. It is a positive, proactive group. The NBEF presents the International Bowhunter Education Program (IBEP), taught by carefully selected volunteer instructors who generate 125,000 man-hours each year. The IBEP covers bowhunter responsibilities, proper equipment, safety, game laws, wildlife conservation, survival and first aid, bowhunting techniques and methods, and anti-hunting threats to bowhunting.

NBEF-produced materials are also distributed by state fish and wildlife agencies for use in firearm safety and other courses. Some states have made the IBEP program mandatory for bowhunters, and others are interested in doing so.

The NBEF keeps a high profile through trade shows, national and international workshops, and joint efforts with other organizations. Much of this visibility is felt to be necessary because of the vital role NBEF plays in the fight to preserve the sport. Improving skills and ethics of the average hunter in the field is critical to lowering the statistics for unrecovered game and reducing the im-

pact from animal-rights activists.

The NBEF is an affiliate of the AAF and is endorsed by more than a dozen top national and international sportsmen's organizations.

## Mission Statement

The NBEF works to ensure the future existence of bowhunting through education and bowhunting information programs. Its goal is to perpetuate bowhunting by providing the fundamentals of good, safe bowhunting with an appreciation and respect for the environment, and to maintain the highest standards of the sport.

The educational program instills in bowhunters a responsible attitude, assists them in adopting exemplary behavior toward people, wildlife and the environment.

Motto: "The Future of Bowhunting Depends on Bowhunter Education."

## How to Join

The NBEF is a nonprofit foundation that offers four levels of individual sponsorship and five levels of group sponsorship. It is open to any person, business, association, publisher, guide/outfitter, organization or agency. Contributions are tax deductible.

Individual sponsors receive a quarterly newsletter, decals and access to NBEF materials. Group sponsors may also use the NBEF logo in their literature along with an appropriate explanatory sentence.

Write the NBEF at the address above for information about becoming a sponsor.

## NATIONAL FIELD ARCHERY ASSOCIATION
*31407 Outer I-10*
*Redlands, California 92373*
*www.nfaa-archery.org*

The National Field Archery Association is a nonprofit corporation dedicated to the practice of archery. Founded in 1939, it is the world's largest archery association with 50 chartered state associations and more than 1,000 affiliated clubs in the U.S. and other countries. It is a member of the International Field Archery Association (IFAA), the world's governing body for field archery.

The NFAA establishes shooting regulations, holds tournaments, maintains records and provides organized state associations and archery clubs with a well-rounded schedule of events. There are events and programs for Youth and Club members, who have the opportunity to earn progressive merit patches as they advance in skill levels.

NFAA bowhunter programs offer recognition through awarding pins and certificates, and shooting skills can earn individuals a place on the 500 Club or the Perfect Club.

The events include national indoor/outdoor championship tournaments, a 3-D national tournament, shooting and equipment clinics, team events, a certified instructor school, sectional and state tournaments, indoor/ outdoor leagues, and in indoor/outdoor Mail-in Match.

### How to Join
The NFAA offers four levels of membership for individuals and three levels for families. All members receive a subscription to *Archery Magazine*, are eligible for NFAA-sponsored hunting award contests and have access to various types of insurance. NFAA members are also members of the IFAA and may compete in the IFAA World Championship. For a membership application, write to the address given above. Telephone: 800-811-2331.

## NATIONAL SHOOTING SPORTS FOUNDATION, INC.
*383 Main Avenue*
*Norwalk, CT 06851*
*www.nssf.org*

The National Shooting Sports Foundation is a nonprofit, educational, trade-supported association founded in 1960 whose interests cover all aspects of shooting. It was the NSSF that originated National Hunting & Fishing Day (officially proclaimed by Congress in 1972) as a means for recognizing the sportsman's contribution to wildlife conservation and to promote a better understanding of and more active participation in the shooting sports.

It was also the NSSF that originated the concept of a trade show dedicated to shooting, hunting and related outdoor industries. The inaugural SHOT Show was held in January 1979 in St. Louis, and the event now ranks as the 33rd largest trade exposition in the U.S. among the 8,000 shows held annually.

The SHOT Show provides manufacturers, dealers and distributors with a marketplace and creates additional revenue for the NSSF programs promoting increased participation in shooting sports. Archery is one of the merchandise categories.

### Mission Statement
NSSF was formed to create in the public mind a better understanding of and a more active participation in the shooting sports and in practical conservation.

### How to Join
The NSSF welcomes participation by individuals and organizations in NHF Day. For information, write to "National Hunting Fishing Day" at the NSSF address listed above.

For complete rules and regulations governing competitive archery, the NSSF recommends contacting the National Archery Association, the National Field Archery Association (both featured in this section) and Bowhunters Silhouettes International, P.O. Box 6470, Orange, CA 92667.

## NORTH AMERICAN HUNTING CLUB
*12301 Whitewater Drive*
*Minnetonka, Minnesota 55343*
*www.huntingclub.com*

The North American Hunting Club began in 1978 when

founder Paul Burke and his son Steve, avid outdoorsmen, decided hunters like themselves needed better information to make them more successful in the field.

The club's popularity skyrocketed with the first editions of its magazine *North American Hunter*. In April 1992, it began a weekly TV show, *North American Outdoors*, telecast to 58 million households on ESPN. The goal of the TV show is "to create a more knowledgeable audience with reinforced high ethical standards."

Club activities include: a computerized outfitter and guide rating service, outfitter-sponsored discounts on great hunting adventures, field testing and review of outdoor products, annual Big-Game Awards contest and President's Trophy, and chances to win free outfitted big-game hunts and outdoor products.

Though the club is not a bowhunters-only organization, it includes emphasis on bowhunting.

**Mission Statement**

The foremost goal of NAHC is to accurately portray hunters in the way that appeals most to ethical, dedicated sportsmen. It places special importance on getting members together to share their passion for hunting, and does all it can to recognize members' successes. To that end, it provides a forum for swap hunts.

**How to Join**

Write to the above address, or call 1-800-922-4868. (The umbrella organization, North American Outdoor Group, also sponsors the North American Fishing Club.)

**POPE & YOUNG CLUB**
*15 2nd Street S.E.*
*Chatfield, Minnesota 55923*
*pope-young.org*

The Pope & Young Club began in 1957 as a part of the National Field Archery Association's Hunting Activities Committee. It was named in honor of pioneer bowhunters Dr. Saxton Pope and Arthur Young, whose exploits early in the 20th century drew national attention to the sport. In 1963 it became a separate incorporated scientific, nonprofit organization, patterned after the prestigious Boone & Crockett Club. P&Y records the finest trophies of North American big game taken with the bow and arrow. The club conducts ongoing recording periods, and every two years it presents appropriate awards for the finest trophies submitted, honoring the skulls, horns or antlers of various trophy-class big-game species.

The club is recognized worldwide as the official repository for bowhunting records. Its highest award is the ISHI Award, named for Ishi, the last surviving member of the Yana Indian tribe of northern California, a friend and bowhunting companion of Dr. Pope and Arthur Young. It is given only when a truly outstanding North American big-game trophy animal is deemed deserving of special recognition.

Pope & Young Club publications are available to individuals, wildlife agencies and conservation organizations.

**Mission Statement**

The Pope & Young Club has grown to epitomize sportsmanship and fair chase hunting. Today it fosters and nourishes bowhunting excellence and encourages responsible bowhunting by promoting quality hunting and sound conservation practices.

The club remains dedicated to the perpetuation and sound management of wild animals and their habitat, as well as other beneficial wildlife practices. Members work actively behind the scenes, quietly supporting various educational, field research and game management programs with moral and financial backing. The club's Conservation Committee investigates and selects worthy projects. In recent years financial grants totaling many thousands of dollars have been awarded in support of habitat preservation, big-game relocation, field research programs and educational projects.

**How to Join**

There are three classifications of membership: Associate, Regular and Senior. All new members must join as an Associate, and to qualify for membership the applicant must have taken, under the Rules of Fair Chase, one adult North American big-game animal with a bow and arrow. Regular and Senior Memberships have additional requirements.

For additional information, write the club at the address given.

## PROFESSIONAL BOWHUNTERS SOCIETY
P.O. Box 206
Terrell, NC 28682
www.bowsite.com/pbs
The Professional Bowhunters Society is an organization of experienced bowhunters. It is a fraternity, or brotherhood, of some of the best bow-hunters in the world. The term "professional" indicates a professional attitude and skill level. The group is dedicated to the belief that personal satisfaction in the sport must be measured in direct relation to the degree of challenge involved—in the hunting, more than the shooting.

PBS was founded in 1963 by 17 accomplished bowhunters who wanted an organization that would serve the particular interests of serious bowhunters, most notably the need for bow weight requirements in target accuracy tests. The late Tom Shupienis, one of the founders, had this vision: "I see no reason why we cannot someday be the prime source of intelligent opinions and sophisticated respect in all matters relative to bowhunting's future, and PBS standards will be the goals of all bowhunters everywhere."

PBS has been active in important and controversial issues. Committees work in the areas of conservation, legislation, publicity and education. It sponsors a National Affiliation Program serving state bowhunters' organizations and performing as an information clearinghouse.

*Bowhunter Magazine* is the official publication of the PBS.

### Mission Statement
The PBS is dedicated to the advancement and preservation of bowhunting as a major outdoor sport. It encourages development of skill in bowhunting and the exchange of knowledge between bowhunters. Members work to improve the overall quality of all bowhunters, to understand their weapons, their capabilities, and to get the maximum effective performance from them.

### How to Join
There are two levels of membership. Regular membership is limited to 500. Applicants must be 21 or older and must satisfy requirements dictating minimums for bow draw weight, arrow weight and game taken. Furthermore, bowhunting, rather than target archery must be the applicant's primary interest. Associate membership is unlimited, and game kill requirements do not apply. Contact the address above for an application form. Telephone:704-664-2534.

## SAFARI CLUB INTERNATIONAL
4800 West Gates Pass Road
Tucson, AZ 85745-9645
www.safariclub.org
Safari Club International was founded in 1971 when C. J. McElroy, then living in Inglewood, California, organized four Safari Club chapters in the Los Angeles area. Since then, it has become a truly international organization representing more than a million hunters worldwide. SCI and its chapters have contributed millions of dollars to projects directly and indirectly benefiting wildlife.

SCI members are vitally interested in preserving the tradition of hunting. To introduce high-school-age youth to wildlife management principles, the organization conducts the SCI American Wilderness Leadership School at Granite Ranch in Wyoming. The SCI Wildlife Museum is another educational tool at the World Headquarters in Tucson, Arizona, and the club has an active wildlife conservation education program that reaches thousands of school children and adults across the Southwest and in northern Mexico. Many SCI chapters participate in Sensory Safaris, where visually impaired children get their first "glimpse" of wildlife. SCI chapters and members are also deeply involved in governmental affairs at local, national and international levels.

Among the currently sponsored conservation projects are management and reintroduction of many species in North and South America, and in Africa.

Camaraderie is important in this organization, and the annual SCI Convention in Las Vegas is well publicized and draws attendees from all over the world.

**Mission Statement**
To promote conservation of the wildlife of the world as a valuable renewable resource in which hunting is one management tool among many; to stimulate conservation education programs and teacher training workshops emphasizing the wise use of renewable natural resources; to educate the public about the importance of wildlife conservation and the role of hunting in proper management of wildlife.

**How to Join**
Write Safari Club International for information about joining or about local chapters in your area. Telephone: 520-620-1220.

**THE WILDLIFE LEGISLATIVE FUND OF AMERICA**
*801 Kingsmill Parkway Columbus, Ohio 43229-1137 www.wlfa.org*
The Wildlife Legislative Fund of America (founded in 1978) is an association of organizations dedicated to protecting the rights of sportsmen to hunt, trap and fish. It represents hundreds of sportsmen's clubs, in all benefiting over 750,000 American sportsmen with its legal, legislative and public relations expertise at the local, state and national levels.

The major effort is a program called "Protect What's Right," endorsed by mainline conservation organizations, the Department of the Interior and fish and wildlife agencies all over America.

The WLFA newsletter, *Update*, regularly incorporates "Bowhunter Defense Coalition NEWS." The WLFA Bowhunter Defense Coalition is a fast-growing arm that includes two dozen national member organizations (major bowhunting clubs and national publications) and over 45 state members. The WLFA is very active in providing training workshops in government and media relations to bowhunter leaders through the BDC.

The organization operates in 500 communities and 50 states, in Congress and the courts. It is active in state and federal wildlife regulatory processes and is waging a nationwide campaign to get the truth about our outdoor heritage to the uninformed public. To this end, it has been on the scene for outdoorsmen in ballot issue campaigns, legislative lobbying efforts and courtroom defenses. It operates a State Services Division, a National Affairs Office in Washington, D.C., a Legal Services Department, and a Public Relations Department.

WLFA provides training to member organizations in five areas. The Media Program offers a complete package of informational materials for use in all media. The Youth Program focuses on audio/visual materials that emphasize conservation with

a pro-hunting slant. The Speakers Bureau Program covers everything from booking speeches to giving them and provides materials that assure a polished presentation. The Legislative Program is a full-scale program that deals with getting to know legislators and how to launch lobbying campaigns.

**Mission Statement**
The Wildlife Legislative Fund of America takes as its sole goal the preservation of our outdoor heritage. Today, our wildlife and our sports are under attack. A tide of government actions in the states and in Washington, D.C., threatens the very foundations of conservation. So that fathers and sons may continue to enjoy days afield, America's conservationists are protecting their legacy through the WLFA.

**How to Join**
Membership is open to both concerned individuals and clubs (which become associate organizations). By joining, members become part of a national network of sportsmen's clubs and take full advantage of an ongoing program that represents sportsmen's issues at the local, state and national levels. All members receive the quarterly newsletter *Update* and legislative *Action Alerts*, and have direct access WLFA staff. Contact WLFA at the address above for additional membership information. Telephone: 614-888-4868.

# Appendix B

# GOVERNMENT REGULATING AGENCIES

The following listings give addresses of state agencies in the U.S. and agencies in the Canadian provinces. (Source: National Wildlife Federation.)

## STATE AGENCIES

**Alabama Dept. of Conservation**
Division of Game and Fish
64 North Union Street
Montgomery, AL 36130
http://www.dcnr.state.al.us/agfd/

**Alaska Dept. of Fish & Game**
P.O. Box 3-2000
Juneau, AK 99802
http://www.state.ak.us/local/ak
    pages/FISH.GAME/adfgho
    me.htm

**Arizona Game & Fish**
2222 West Greenway Road
Phoenix, AZ 85023
http://www.gf.state.az.us/
    welcome.html

**Arkansas Game & Fish Commission**
#2 Natural Resources Drive
Little Rock, AR 72205
http://www.state.ar.us/

**California Dept. of Fish & Game**
1416 9th Street
Sacramento, CA 95814
http://www.dfg.ca.gov/

**Colorado Division of Wildlife**
6060 Broadway
Denver, CO 80216
http://www.dnr.state.co.us/
    wildlife/hunt/index.asp

**Connecticut Dept. of Environmental Protection**
State Office Bldg., 165 Capitol Avenue
Hartford, CT 06115
http://dep.state.ct.us/pao/index.
    htm

**Delaware Division of Fish and Wildlife**
P.O. Box 1401
Dover, DE 19903
http://www.dnrec.state.de.us/fw/
    fwwel.htm

**Florida Game and Freshwater Fish Commission**
Farris Bryant Building
620 South Meridian
Tallahassee, FL 32399
http://www.state.fl.us/fwc/
    hunting/hunting.html

Georgia State Game and Fish
Division
Floyd Towers East, Suite 1366
205 Butler Street, S.E.
Atlanta, GA 30334
http://www.dnr.state.ga.us/

Division of Forestry & Wildlife
1151 Punch Bowl Street
Honolulu, HI 96813
http://mano.icsd.hawaii.gov/
dlnr/dcre/know.htm

Idaho Fish & Game
Department
600 S. Walnut, P.O. Box 25
Boise, ID 83707
http://www2.state.id.us/
fishgame/fishgame.html

Illinois Dept. of Conservation
Lincoln Tower Plaza
524 South 2nd Street
Springfield, IL 62701-1787
http://dnr.state.il.us/

Indiana Div. of Fish and
Wildlife
607 State Office Building
Indianapolis, IN 46204
http://www.state.in.us/dnr/
fishwild/index.htm

Iowa Department of Natural
Resources
Wallace State Office Building
East 9th and Grand Avenue
Des Moines, IA 50319
http://www.state.ia.us/
government/dnr/index.html

Kansas Department of Wildlife
and Parks
Box 54-A, Rural Route 2
Pratt, KS 67124
http://www.kdwp.state.ks.us/
hunting/hunting.html

Kentucky Dept. of Fish &
Wildlife Resources
#1 Game Farm Road
Frankfort, KY 40601
http://www.state.ky.us/agencies/
fw/wildlife.htm

Louisiana Dept. Wildlife and
Fisheries
2000 Quail Drive, P.O. Box
98000
Baton Rouge, LA 70898
http://www.wlf.state.la.us/

Maine Dept. of Inland Fisheries
& Wildlife
284 State Street, Station #41
Augusta, ME 04333
http://www.state.me.us/ifw/
index.html

Maryland Department of
Natural Resources
Tawes State Office Building
Annapolis, MD 21401
http://www.dnr.state.md.us/
huntersguide/

Massachusetts Div. of Fisheries
& Wildlife
Department of Fisheries,
Wildlife and Environmental
Law Enforcement
100 Cambridge Street
Boston, MA 02202
http://www.state.ma.us/dfwele/
dfw/dfwrec.htm

Michigan Dept. of Natural
Resources
Stevens T. Mason Bldg., Box
30028
Lansing, MI 48909
http://www.dnr.state.mi.us/

Minnesota Dept. of Natural
Resources
500 Lafayette Road
St. Paul, MN 55155-4020
http://www.dnr.state.mn.us/
hunting.html

Mississippi Dept. of Wildlife,
Fisheries and Parks
P.O. Box 451
Jackson, MS 39205
http://www.mdwfp.com/hunting
.asp

Missouri Dept. of Conservation
2901 North Ten Mile Drive,
P.O. Box 180
Jefferson City, MO 65102
http://www.conservation.state.
mo.us/

Montana Dept. of Fish,
Wildlife, and Parks
1420 East 6th Avenue
Helena, MT 59620
http://www.fwp.state.mt.us/hun
ting/hunting.htm

Nebraska Game & Parks
Commission
2200 North 33rd Street, P.O.
Box 30370
Lincoln, NE 68503
http://164.119.102.21/
hunting/hunting.html

Nevada Department of Wildlife
P.O. Box 10678
Reno, NV 89520
http://nevadadivisionofwildlife.
org/

New Hampshire Fish and Game
Department
2 Hazen Drive
Concord, NH 03301
http://www.wildlife.state.nh.us/
hunting.html

New Jersey Div. of Fish, Game
and Wildlife
CN 400
Trenton, NJ 08625
http://www.state.nj.us/dep/fgw/
hunting.htm

New Mexico Game and Fish
Department
Villagra Building
Santa Fe, NM 87503
http://www.gmfsh.state.nm.us/

New York Division of Fish and
Wildlife
50 Wolf Road
Albany, NY 12233
http://www.dec.state.ny.us/

North Carolina Wildlife
Resources Commission
512 North Salisbury Street
Raleigh, NC 27611
http://www.state.nc.us/Wildlife/

North Dakota Game & Fish
Department
100 North Bismark Expressway
Bismark, ND 58501
http://www.state.nd.us/gnf/

Ohio Division of Wildlife
Fountain Square
Columbus, OH 43224
http://www.dnr.state.oh.us/

Oklahoma Dept. of Wildlife
Conservation
1801 North Lincoln, P.O. Box 53465
Oklahoma City, OK 73152
http://www.state.ok.us/

Oregon Dept. of Fish & Wildlife
P.O. Box 59
Portland, OR 97207
http://www.dfw.state.or.us/

Pennsylvania Game Commission
2001 Elmerton Avenue
Harrisburg, PA 17110-9797
http://www.dcnr.state.pa.us/

Puerto Rico Department of Natural Resources
P.O. Box 5887
Puerta De Tierra
San Juan, PR 00906

Rhode Island Dept. of Environmental Management
Division of Fish and Wildlife
Washington County Government Center
Wakefield, RI 02879
http://www.huntri.com/home.shtml

South Carolina Wildlife & Marine Resources Dept.
Rembert C. Dennis Bldg., P.O. Box 167
Columbia, SC 29202
http://www.dnr.state.sc.us/etc/hunting.html

South Dakota Dept. of Game, Fish and Parks
Sigurd Anderson Building, 445 East Capitol
Pierre, SD 57501-3185
http://www.state.sd.us/gfp/hunting/INDEX.HTM

Tennessee Wildlife Resources Agency
Ellington Agricultural Center, P.O. Box 40747
Nashville, TN 37204
http://www.state.tn.us/twra/hunt001b2.html

Texas Parks & Wildlife Department
4200 Smith School Road
Austin, TX 78744
http://www.tpwd.state.tx.us/hunt/hunt.htm

Utah Division of Wildlife Resources
1596 West North Temple
Salt Lake City, UT 84116
http://www.nr.state.ut.us/

Vermont Fish & Game Department
103 S. Main Street, 10 South
Waterbury, VT 05676
http://www.anr.state.vt.us/fw/fwhome/

Virginia Dept. of Game and Inland Fisheries
4010 West Broad Street, P. O. Box 11104
Richmond, VA 23230
http://www.dgif.state.va.us/hunting/index.cfm

Washington Department of Wildlife
600 North Capitol Way
Olympia, WA 98504
http://www.wa.gov/wdfw/huntcorn.htm

West Virginia Div. of Wildlife Resources
1900 Kanawha Blvd. East
Charleston, WV 25305
http://www.state.wv.us/dnr/wvhunting/

Wisconsin Dept. of Natural Resources
Box 7921
Madison, WI 53707
http://www.dnr.state.wi.us/

Wyoming Game & Fish Department
5400 Bishop Blvd.
Cheyenne, WY 82002
http://gf.state.wy.us/

AGENCIES IN CANADIAN PROVINCES

ALBERTA
Director of Wildlife
Fish and Wildlife Division
Department of Energy and Natural Resources
Petroleum Plaza, South Tower
9945-108 Street
Edmonton, Alberta
CANADA T5K 2C9
http://www3.gov.ab.ca/srd/fishwl.html

BRITISH COLUMBIA
Director, Wildlife Branch
Ministry of the Environment
Parliament Buildings
Victoria, British Columbia
CANADA V8V 1X5
http://www.gov.bc.ca/wlap/

MANITOBA
Director, Wildlife Branch
Natural Resources Division
Department of Natural Resources
Room 302, Legislative Building
Winnipeg, Manitoba
CANADA R3C 0V8
http://www.gov.mb.ca/natres/index.html

NEW BRUNSWICK
Director
Fish and Wildlife Branch
Department of Natural Resources
Centennial Bldg., P.O. Box 6000
Fredericton, New Brunswick
CANADA E3B 5H1
http://www.gnb.ca/0078/Index.htm

## NEWFOUNDLAND

Wildlife Division
Department of Culture,
   Recreation and Youth
P.O. Box 4750
St. Johns, Newfoundland
CANADA A1C 5T7
http://www.gov.nf.ca/tourism/

## NORTHWEST TERRITORY

Chief,
Wildlife Management
   Division
Department of Renewable
   Resources
Legislative Building
Yellowknife, Northwest
   Territory
CANADA X1A 2L9
http://www.nwtwildlife.rwed.
   gov.nt.ca/

## NOVA SCOTIA

Wildlife Division
Department of Lands and
   Forests
Toronto Dominion Bank
   Building
1791 Barrington Street
P.O. Box 698
Halifax, Nova Scotia
CANADA B3J 2T9
http://www.gov.ns.ca/natr/hunt/
   huntregs.htm

## ONTARIO

Wildlife Director
Outdoor Recreation Group
Ontario Ministry of Natural
   Resources
Whitney Block, Queen's Park
Toronto, Ontario
CANADA M7A 1W3
http://www.mnr.gov.on.ca/
   MNR/pubs/pubmenu.html

## PRINCE EDWARD ISLAND

Minister
Community and Cultural
   Affairs
11 Kent Street, P.O. Box 2000
Charlottetown, Prince Edward
   Island
CANADA C1A 7N8
http://www.gov.pe.ca/
   visitorsguide/explore/
   hunting.php3

## QUEBEC

Director,
Fish and Game Branch
Quebec Ministere Du Loisir,
   De La Chasse Ed De La
   Peche
150 est boul, St.-Cyrille
Quebec City, Quebec
CANADA G1R 4Y1
http://www.tourisme.gouv.qc.
   ca/magazine/index_en.asp

## SASKATCHEWAN

Director,
Wildlife Branch
Saskatchewan Park and
   Renewable Resources
Legislative Building
Regina, Saskatchewan
CANADA S4S 5W6
http://www.gov.sk.ca/

## YUKON TERRITORY

Chief of Wildlife Management
Wildlife Branch
Department of Renewable
   Resources
P.O. Box 2703
Whitehorse, Yukon Territory
CANADA Y1A 2C6
http://www.renres.gov.yk.ca

# INDEX

accessories, 13, 30–31, 30–33, 33–34
  for big-game hunting, 88–97, 89–92,
    94–96
  calls, 104–6, 105–6
  camouflage, 97–98, 97–100, 100
  scents, 101–3, 102–3
  for wild turkey hunting, 146–47
accuracy, 58, 84, 131, 159, 174
*Adventurous Bowmen, The* (Pope), 6, 81
African big game, 80–82, 107
aim, 45, 46–47, 47–50, 49–50
air friction, 18
Alaskan brown bear, 72, 72–73
alcoholic beverages, 61
alignment devices, 25
aluminum arrows, 18, 22, 25, 163
aluminum/carbon composite arrows,
    22–23
anchor point, 43, 44

antelope, 8, 123
antihunting sentiment, xii, 59
archer's paradox, 18
archery/bowhunting
  clubs, 35
  government regulating agencies,
    185–88
  history of, ix–xi, 167
  organizations, 177–84
archery competitions, 167–72, 168–71
  NAA and NFAA events, 172, 173,
    174
  Olympic archery, 174
  world target archery, 175
arm guards, 31, 33
armadillos, 159
arrow rests, 11, 88–89, 89
arrows, 15, 17–18
  broadheads, 26, 26–29, 27

arrows *(cont.)*
  erratic flight of, 51–52
  fiberglass, 162, 163, *165*
  fletching, 22, 23, 23–24
  flu-flu, 149–50
  length of, 15
  making your own, 25
  matching to draw length, 29
  materials, 18–23
  points for practice & small game,
      25–26
  shaft size selection, 19–21

backpacks, *91*
badgers, 159
Bear, Fred, 4, 6
  in Africa, 81–82
  polar bear hunting and, 74–75
  recurve bows and, 15
  on step-across method, 38–39
beaver, 158, *158*
bedding areas, 124, 125
big game, 16, 63–64, 83–84
  accessories for hunting, 88–106,
      *89–92, 94–98, 100, 102–3,*
      *105–6*
  field dressing, 86–87
  shooting to kill, 84–86
  using meat of, 87–88
  *See also individual species*
bighorn sheep, 76, *76*
binoculars, 90, 92, 122, 123, 146
birds, 24, 26, 30, *147–48, 147–51, 151*
  *See also* wild turkey
black bear, *71,* 71–72, 153
blacktail deer, 65–66
blinds, 98, 117, 142, 155
blunt points, 25
boar, 80
boats, 135, 163, 165
bobcat, *156,* 156–57
bolts, 13
boots, 121, *121*
bow cases, 34

bow slings, 33
bow squares, 34, 39, 40
bowfishing, 26, 161–63, *163–65,*
      165–66
bows
  bracing, 37–39
  compound, *8,* 8–10, *9, 11,* 12
  crossbow, 11–13, *13*
  longbow, 4–6, *5,* 12
  recurve bow, 6, 7
bowsights, *11,* 45, 47, 49–50, *49–50*
bowstrings, 34, 39
brace height, 39, 39–40
breath camouflage, 100
broadhead arrows, 26, *26–29, 27,* 48, 93
  for game birds, 151
  removal from dead animals, 86
  safety precautions and, 52
  for wild turkey hunting, *140,* 146
buck boards, 106
buddy system, 56
bullfrogs, 135
bull's-eye targets, 30

calls, 104–6, *105–6,* 143–45, *144–45,*
      155–56, 157
camouflage, 75, 97–98, *97–100, 100,*
      110, 140, 142, *142*
campfires, 61
cams, 9–10, *10*
Canada goose, 149, *151*
carbon arrows, 18, 22
caribou, 68–70, *69,* 130
carp, 161, 163, 166
Cascade Release, 31
clay pigeons, 150
climbing tree stands, *111,* 111–12
clothing, 48, 56, 99, 120–21, *121*
Clout, 170
cock feather, 24
compasses, 125
compound bows, *8,* 8–10, *9, 11,* 12
  in archery competitions, 169
  arrow shaft size and, 19–20

arrow weight and, 15
brace height, 40
draw length and, 29
draw weight and, 16
holding/aiming with, 43, *43*
popularity of, 13
for use by youngsters, *34*, 34–35
for wild turkey hunting, 145
cord bowstringers, 34
cord stringers, 37
coyote, 153–56, *154*
crossbows, 11–13, *13*
crowding, 60
crows, 159
cushions, 94

daypacks, 55
distance, estimating, 48
dogs, hunting with, 78, 134
drag, 23, 164
draw length, 29
draw weight, 8, 15, 16, 34
drawing, 42–43, 51
driving, 127–30, *129*
droppings, 124
dry-firing, 52

elk, *67*, 67–68, 105, 118, 123, 130
emergency kits, 97
English bow, 5
equipment, 1–3
    arrows, 17–30, 22–23, 26–27
    basic accessories, 30–31, *30–33*,
        33–34
    bow selection & bow weight, 15–16
    bow types, 4–6, *5*, *7–13*, *8–13*
    ethics and, 58
    master eye and, 3–4
    preferences in, 13–15, *14*
    for wild turkey hunting, 145–46
    for youngsters, *34*, 34–35
ethics, 57–62, *59*

feathers, 23, 24, 48

Fédération Internationale de Tir à l'Arc
    (FITA), 175
feral boar, 80
fiberglass arrows, 18, 22, 162, 163, *165*
field dressing game, 86–87, 92
field games, 167
field points, 25, 151
finger release, 33, 40, 47, *47*
fire tracks, 95
first aid kits, 54, 55, 96
fish, 161–63, 165–66
fixed blades, 27, 28
flashlights, 92
fletching, 17, 22, 23, *23–24*, 163
flip-over targets, 30
flu-flu arrows, 24, 149–50
follow-through, 45, *45*
foxes, *155*, 156
friction calls, 143
Frisbees, target practice with, 150,
    *150*
frog hunting, 24, 135

game, 58–59, 61, 78
    *See also* big game; small game;
    *individual species*
game trackers, 94–95
gap shooting, 47, 48
gar, 163, 165, 166
Global Positioning System (GPS), 96,
    125
gloves, 30, 33, 42
grabbers, 26
grand slam, 76
gravity, 18
greasepaint, 100
grizzly bear, *73*, 73–74
groundhog, *157*, 157–58
grouse, 147–48, *148*, 151
grunt calls, 104, 106

hand gaffs, 165
hen feathers, 24
holding and aiming, *43*, 43–44

*Hunting with the Bow and Arrow*
(Pope), x, 6
Hyde, Tony, 172
hypothermia, 54–56

Indian tribes, x, 4, 5
insect and tick repellent, 96–97, 136
instinctive shooting, 47–48, 149

Jacobsen, Rockie, 171–72
javelina, 134
judo points, 26

kinetic energy, 17
kisser buttons, 174
Knight, Harold, 48
knives, 92, 94, *94*

ladder tree stands, 114
landowners, 59–60, 61–62
laws/regulations, xi, 59, 108, 111, 138,
    149
  bowfishing and, 162, 166
  government regulating agencies,
    185–88
  protected species, 153
  varmint hunting, 159
Lee, Ben Rodgers, 142
let-off, 8
lights/lighting conditions, 50, 95–96
longbows, 4–6, *5*, 12
  accessories for, 34
  arrow weight and, 15
  brace height, 39
  draw length and, 29
  draw weight and, 16
  holding/aiming with, 43

master eye, 3–4
mechanical heads, 27; 28
moose, 79, *79*, 93, 105
mountain goat, 77, *77*
mountain lion, 78, *78*
mouth calls, 143–44

mule deer, 65–66, *66*, 93, 105, 123

National Archery Association, x, 172,
    174, 179–80
National Bowhunter Education
    Foundation (NBEF), 35
National Field Archery Association
    (NFAA), 172, 174, 181
nock locators, 25
nocks/nocking, 34, 40, *40*, 42, 52
noise, 10
North American sheep, 76, 76–77

offensive behavior, 61
Olympics, x, 174
oppossums, 134

pack horses, 68
peccary, 134
peep sights, *50*, 90, *91*
pendulum sights, 49–50
penetration, 17, 28, 151
pin sights, 49, *49*
plastic vanes, as fletching, 23–24
point-of-aim, 47
points, on arrows, 25–26
polar bear, *74*, 74–75
polarized sunglasses, 166
Pope, Saxon, x–xi, 4, 5, 6, 80–81
porcupines, 159
prairie dog, 158, *159*
pro shops, 2–3
pronghorn antelope, *75*, 75–76

quivers, *11*, 32, 33–34

rabbits, 131–33, *133*
raccoons, 134, *134*
rangefinders, 90–91, *92*, 146
rattling, 104, *105*, *106*
recurve bows, 6, *7*
  accessories for, 34
  arrow shaft size and, 19–20
  arrow weight and, 15

draw length and, 29
draw weight and, 16
holding/aiming with, 43
in Olympic competition, 174
releases, mechanical, 31, 33, 40, 42, 44,
    88, 88
repair kits, 34
replaceable blades, 26, 27–28
ringneck pheasants, 147, 147, 149, 151
Robin Hood, 168
rod and reel, 163, 164
ruffed grouse, 148, 148

safety precautions, 35, 52–56, 53, 75,
    78, 109, 115–16, 130
sage grouse, 147, 148
saws, 91–92, 94
scents, 101–3, 102–3
Schuh, Dwight, 55
scope sights, 12–13, 49, 49
scouting, 141
scrapes, 124
sharks, 166
sharpening tools, 28
shooting
    aiming aids, 45, 46–47, 47–50, 49–50
    brace height, 39, 39–40
    bracing the bow, 37–39
    improving aim, 50
    nocking point, 40, 40
    steps to achieving skill, 41, 41–45,
        43–45
shooting lanes, 109, 114
shooting to kill, 84–86, 93
signal fires, 54
single-cam designs, 8, 9
skunks, 159
small game, 25, 26, 131–35, 133, 134
smoke signals, 54
snow goose, 149
sound amplifiers, 94, 95
specialty arrows, 24
spine, 17
sportsmanship, 59

spruce grouse, 148, 148
squirrels, 119, 133–34
stabilizers, 11, 89–90, 90
stalking, 117, 154
    bad weather, 120
    clothing for, 120–21, 121
    knowing the terrain, 122–25
    moving quietly, 118–19, 119
    wind direction and, 119–20, 120
stance, 41, 41–42, 51
starlings, 159
step-across method, 37–39
stick bows, 15
stiffness, 17
stingray, 166
straighteners, 25
strap-on tree stands, 112–13, 112–13
string silencers, 11, 31
string walking, 47, 48, 49
stringkeepers, 34
survey tape, 94

tabs, 30, 33
target practice, 29, 30–31, 50, 58, 84,
    150, 171
thinhorn sheep, 76
Thompson brothers, x, 5
3-D targets, 168–70, 170–71, 172
three-fingers-under shooting method,
    47, 48–49
thumbtacks, 94
ticks, 96
tool kits, 97
tree stands, 9, 107–9, 109, 115
    climbing, 111, 111–12
    improvement in, 48
    ladder, 114
    pendulum sights for, 49–50
    safety precautions and, 52–53, 53
    scouting and placement of, 108, 110
    strap-on, 112–13, 112–13
    tripod, 114–16
tripod tree stands, 114–16
trophies, 61, 76, 82

turkey. *See* wild turkey
two-cam designs, 9

U.S. Fish and Wildlife Service, 149

varmints, 153–59, *154–59*
vibration, 10

wading, 165
Wand, 170
weather, 54, 120
West, Don, 172
wheel design, 9–10, *10*
whitetail deer, *64*, 64–65, 98–99, 102, 105, 123
wild boar, 80
wild turkey, 98–99, 109, 118, 137–38, *139*
  accessories for hunting, 146–47
  calls, 143–45, *144–45*

equipment and shooting, 145–46
hunting tactics for, 139–43
species of, 138–39
wildlife management, 60
wind direction, 110, 119–20, *120*, 128
wingshooting, 149–51, *150*, *151*
women, archery/bowhunting and, *14*, 174, 175
woodchuck, 157
wooden arrows, 18, 48, 163
woodsmanship, 142–43
wrist, position of, 42
wrist slings, *11*
wrist straps, 32

Young, Art, x, 4, 5, 6, 80–81
youngsters, equipment and instruction for, 2, 4, 13, *34*, 34–35
Yukon roving, 170–71